Charis-Magic
In Public Speaking:
The Power
To Move People

Charis-Magic In Public Speaking: The Power To Move People

Dick Milham

Parker Publishing Company, Inc.
West Nyack, New York

Library of Congress Cataloging in Publication Data

Milham, Dick
    Charis-magic in public speaking.

    Includes index.
    1. Public Speaking. I. Title.
PN4121.M55655   808.5'1   79-24509
ISBN 0-13-128264-6

Introduction

What Charis-Magic
Can Do For You

★charisma:	that rare quality attributed to people who have dynamic leadership ability and who inspire great devotion in others.
★magic:	the power to produce effects that seem more than human.
★Charis-magic:	the power to move people.

··

When was the last time you heard a speaker who had the power to grip you in his magic? In a world interwoven with billion dollar communication systems, why should only a handful of speakers possess this power to effectively move an audience?

What makes the difference? What magnetic force so energizes them that you can't help but be drawn into their presentations? What causes them to stand out from all the rest?

Certainly it is not a lack of desire on the part of the speakers themselves. Over and over I have heard:

"If I could only discover the secret of shaking up an audience. If I could just see people moved to cheers or tears or rise to their feet. What is it going to take to make me a dynamic, spellbinding after-dinner speaker?"

For years I've heard speakers from the platform try to make me feel better by saying that this magic is born in a person and can't be learned. I was led to believe that it was a special gift bestowed on just a few.

Not so!

The very purpose of this book is to show a speaker, and maybe a good one at that, how to add a magic touch that will make the difference between giving a good speech and receiving a standing ovation.

In these pages you will discover the secret of Charis-magic power; the secret of how you can be endowed with a persuasive power that will revolutionize your ability to arouse an audience.

Some have likened this power to a kind of magic potion that is given to the audience. The analogy is not a bad one. In the opening chapters you discover the psychological ingredients that go into brewing the potion. When a speaker offers it, and when an audience drinks it, power becomes possible.

On the practical level of speech preparation, this book contains what I consider to be the finest method of structuring and outlining a speech to generate Charis-magic power.

You will also uncover a gold mine of fresh, relevant illustrations with a way to test them for Charis-magic results.

The book also provides techniques of mental preparation and self-image exercises that will help prepare you personally. And, finally, I will help you bring it all together for your moment of truth—the actual delivery of your speech.

The closing chapter offers you a collection of anecdotes, and motivational and humorous stories. These will also help you add Charis-Magic power to your presentations.

Over the years, I have discovered almost without exception, that if you are a speaker, you probably want to be a better speaker. In a real sense you are a marked person; marked by your striving for excellence—your desire to be the very best.

In that spirit, this book offers the distillation of my whole life in the arena of public speaking. May you be rewarded with the exhilaration that comes from having an audience in the palm of your hand. May you see them come to their feet in a confirmation of your possession of power—Charis-magic power, the power to move people.

Dick Milham

Contents

Chapter Three

*Five "Assurances" That Guarantee
Charis-Magic Results * 49*

Chapter Four

*How to Develop a Charis-Magic Personality * 63*

Chapter Five

*The Charis-Magic Power of Showing
You're a Pro in the Know * 81*

Chapter Six

The Charis-Magic Impact of Speaking Sincerely * 97

Chapter Seven

Express Your Feelings With Charis-Magic Results * 115

Chapter Eight

Applying Charis-Magic To Human Need and Greed * 133

Chapter Nine

How To Structure The Charis-Magic Speech * 149

Chapter Ten

Building Charis-Magic Into Your Content * 165

Chapter Eleven

How To Meet and Speak To Your Audience With
Charis-Magic Impact * 183

Chapter Twelve

Unleashing Charis-Magic Energy * 199

Chapter Thirteen
A Charis-Magic Treasure Chest * 209

A collection of anecdotes and motivational and humorous
stories.

 One

Uncovering the Secret
of
Charis-Magic Power

From the viewpoint of the speaker, Charis-magic power depends on two psychological conditions:

1. Your own expectation of power.
2. Your ability to build a trust relationship with the audience.

This chapter deals with the first condition, your own expectation of power as a public speaker, and shares proven techniques of "stretching" that expectation to include the possibility of Charis-magic power.

EXPECT CHARIS-MAGIC POWER NOW!

Many speakers feel that power in public speaking can only come as the end result of long searching and preparing, but this is just not the case. You don't have to wait until you've piled up years of speaking experiences or developed some unusual technical skills. Power in your speaking can begin right now!

Power is not simply the result of how well you pronounce words, or string your sentences together, or gesture with your hands. Granted, these all have importance and certainly add to your refinement as a speaker; but *persuasive power is more than a series of speech techniques!* In fact, sometimes power will erupt with stunning effects in the unsteady presentation of a beginner.

One of the most stirring moments I have ever witnessed of this phenomenon came while participating in a telethon to raise money for muscular dystrophy. During a particular segment of the telecast, the camera moved in for a close shot of a middle-aged woman in a wheelchair. The studio lights were nearly blinding her, but she looked into the camera and after a long moment said:

"I am dying, and only you can help me."

For the next ten minutes, those of us in the studio were mesmerized. Her words were faltering, her thoughts were out of sequence, but she had a message and she delivered it with power. Technically, she would have scored low on a speech exam, but power is more than doing the right things technically.

Frustration has plagued many speakers because they have been led to believe that they would find persuasive power in their presentations if they just learned the proper methods. So they have worked, practiced and studied the suggested procedures; as a result, many have become excellent speakers, but not *powerful* ones.

Charis-magic power, by its very nature, does not spring merely from techniques, nor is it dependent on them. You can experience power *now* regardless of your level of speaking expertise! Once this awareness that power can be yours *now* becomes an expectation, you are on your way to experiencing it.

THE AMAZING EXPECTATION OF THE CHARIS-MAGIC SPEAKER

What makes the difference between just another speaker and a powerful one? Why can two people deliver the same speech with basically the same content and one of them puts you to sleep and the other keeps you glued to the edge of your seat?

This intriguing question came up during a seminar I was leading with about a dozen executives who had done their share of public speaking. The discussion heated up almost immediately and soon the air was charged with conflicting opinions.

One executive argued almost vehemently that the difference in speakers could be accounted for by the quality of the voice. In an article he had read, the author speculated that a low-voiced speaker has greater power over his audiences than a person with a high-pitched voice.

"It's a matter of conditioning," he argued. "Since we were kids we identified maturity and authority with the sounds that came out of the mouths of the adults around us; and compared to our little squeeks, they had booming, low voices."

Another man pondered that the key to the puzzle might be found in the actual rhythm of the words as they were spoken. He mentioned how tests have shown that under certain conditions the tempo of spoken words can have an almost hypnotic effect on the listeners.

Some believed that at least some of the answer could be found in the way the speaker used gestures. They pointed to current studies in body language that suggest people can achieve power over others by using certain movements of the body. One older executive, with tongue in cheek, even suggested that the secret might be linked with the time of the full moon.

At the end of about an hour I broke into the discussion and commented, "You know, we have examined just about every alternative but one. In all our debate over what was going on in the speaker's voice and body, none of us asked what was going on in his mind. Let me toss out a thought for your consideration. Could there be some unique process going on in the mind of the persuasive speaker that accounts for his ability to have such a profound impact on his audiences?" The debate was off and running again, hotter then before.

What I have concluded after many years is that the Charis-magic speaker *fully expects powerful things to happen.* From the moment he begins to speak, the air is charged with his conviction that his speech will persuade people. He is a person who delivers his speech in an atmosphere of high expectations. For him there is no question that power will be evidenced through his words.

THE LAW OF EXPECTATION

Charis-magic rests on a law of human nature so charged with energy that when injected into a speaking situation power becomes possible. This law, the law of expectation, implies that *the prerequisite for certain things to happen is your belief that they will happen!* Translated into the speaking arena this means that to have power you must be expecting power.

What do you anticipate is going to happen when you step before an audience? You may be extremely well prepared as far as your material is concerned. Your outline may be excellent and your content stimulating. You may be throughly knowledgeable about your subject matter and confident about your delivery; but what is the state of your mental expectation? How have you prepared your mind?

Before you say a word, do you see in your mind's eye your audience on the edge of their seats, listening and responding to your every word, or are you just hoping to make a decent showing and collect a few compliments? To have power you must be expecting power!

YOU NEVER RISE ABOVE YOUR EXPECTATIONS

This lesson in living with high expectations hit me very forcibly some years ago. Hoping to improve my skills and pick up a few productive ideas, I was attending a seminar in public speaking. One of the lecturers was an established professional with a lot of experience. After one of his sessions I asked him:

"How far can a man go in this speaking business?"

"How far do you want to go?" he questioned.

"Oh, I guess I'd like to make a fairly good living out of it and get to see a lot of the country."

"Is that all," he questioned again.

I thought for a moment and in the insecurity I was feeling at that time replied, "I guess so."

"Well, then," he shot back, "that's all you'll get! Let me leave you with a word of advice. Be careful where you set your goals and expectations in life. There's little chance you're ever going to rise above them!"

Most speakers never experience the exhilaration of a turned-on audience because they never expect to experience it. They have not allowed their expectations to include that possibility.

While working on a consulting assignment in a small insurance company in the west, the sales manager told me how he always left his rallies feeling empty and disappointed in his speaking performance. I asked him, "Before you open your rally what are you expecting to happen? Before you ever step foot into that room do you really believe you're going to have an impact on your sales force?"

"Well, I guess I'm hoping I'll get through to them and really charge them up, but I know it will usually end up the same as every other time."

"But suppose it didn't!" I said. "Suppose that when you got through, your entire sales force jumped up to their feet and started cheering you."

"I'd probably drop dead!" he retorted.

I started him on a program of "stretching" his expectations, a mental exercise you will be introduced to later in this chapter. Slowly he learned to speak with expectation, and eventually achieved the results that had always eluded him.

You will severely handicap yourself as a persuasive speaker if you have not made room in your mind for the possibility of power erupting from your speeches. The problem here is not just one faced by beginners. Many good speakers have never allowed themselves to believe they can become powerful speakers! Sometimes, the reason for this self-imposed limitation rises out of our own self-image. Of necessity, we need to deal with that concept now.

SELF-IMAGE PSYCHOLOGY — THE KEY TO POWER

The discovery of the self-image has been acclaimed by some as the most important psychological discovery of this century. Certainly, this concept helps to explain why some speakers show so much confidence and expectancy in their speeches and why others seem to have a problem.

The self-image is a mental picture of the way you see yourself. It has been put together from all your past experiences, all your successes and failures—all the way from scoring a winning touchdown to striking out with the bases loaded. It has been built out of the opinions and judgments of parents, friends and enemies, all the way from "Stupid, you'll never amount to anything!" to "You're a survivor and a winner. Don't ever quit trying!"

Through the years, from all these bits and pieces, you have mentally constructed a picture of the kind of person you think you are. This picture is in your subconscious mind and even though it may not be clear to you, it is complete in every detail. Once a bit or piece becomes a part of your self-image, once you have accepted it as a "true statement" about the kind of person you are, it begins to exert tremendous influence on your actions and feelings.

You will consistently act like the kind of person you think you are. If you see yourself as a "winner," if you have been fortunate to have the kind of experiences that gave you a healthy self-image, you will always be trying to succeed no matter what the odds.

On the other hand, the person who thinks of himself as a failure, who has built his self-image out of crumbling experiences, will always find a way to fail. Even if the opportunity to succeed were placed right at his feet, he'd find a way to grind it into the ground. Because he sees himself as a failure, he will live a life that is consistent with his failure-image.

The story is told about such a man who, along with two of his companions, was caught during the French Revolution as a suspected enemy of the Republic. Given a hasty trial, they were condemned and led to the guillotine. The first man put his neck into the execution channel and cried out "Vive la France!" as his executioners cut the guillotine loose. It came hurtling down and stopped two inches short of his neck. Feeling the man had suffered enough, his executioners pulled him out and freed him.

The second man swaggered courageously to the guillotine, proud of his part in the Revolution. Again the blade was released and again it stopped short of his neck. He was also freed.

The third man approached the guillotine trembling, thinking about how he always seemed to end up in some kind of mess. Cautiously he put his neck under the guillotine's glistening blade, looked up at the men getting ready to execute him, looked back at the guillotine and then cried out,

"You know something, fellows? If you'd loosen this little screw, this thing would work!"

THE LIMITING-IMAGE

Most of us are not suffering from a failure-image though, and neither are we riding the crest of a success-image all the time. Most of us are simply contending with what I call a limiting-image. Because of our experiences in the past, we have locked into our self-images bits and conclusions about ourselves that limit our abilities, feelings and actions in different areas of our lives.

We feel we deserve happiness, but only so much. We feel that we can make money, but only so much. We know we have the ability to achieve success, but only so much. We are always setting limitations because of certain feelings or hang-ups that might not even be clear to us.

Time and again I have observed this self-limiting image in my work with the business community. During a seminar on "Self-Image and Sales Skills" for an insurance agency in

Chicago, we were discussing the effect of our childhood experiences on our effectiveness in business.

A young man stood up and said, "Okay, I'll play your little game. Tell me something. Why is it that I feel great going into a home to sell some insurance until I get the name on the contract? The minute they sign the papers and hand me their check, I get nervous and want to get out of there as fast as possible.

"Now, that's not the worst of it. I can't seem to ask for referral business from them. When I start asking them to give me some names of their friends and relatives so I can call on them, I get an uneasy feeling."

"But you know," one of his associates cut in, "that referrals are the life blood of this business."

"Yes, I know that. I learned that early and teach it to all my men, but I just can't seem to . . ."

"Larry, let me ask you something," I interrupted, "When you were growing up did your family ever have a bad experience with an insurance company?"

He thought for a moment and then a strange look flashed across his face. "You know, I hadn't thought about it for years, but when I was about seven years old our house burned down. We were wiped out of everything." Suddenly he became very angry.

". . . and do you know that the insurance company ripped us off? I can still hear my parents talking about how they cheated us out of all we had coming, and I can still remember . ."

He stopped and grew very silent, his mind churning over the past, and then he blurted out, "I've been working in a business that down deep I don't believe in. No wonder I've had trouble asking for new business, and break out in a sweat whenever I write a contract on a policy. I feel as if I've been cheating and ripping people off, and I didn't even know I felt that way!"

We spent some time in the seminar discussing his experience, showing how a hidden part of ourselves can play havoc with our ability to cope with life and come into play in our relationship to other people.

After that experience, Larry went on to become one of the

finest managers his company had ever known. By coming to grips with his limiting-image, he was freed to accomplish greater achievements.

Now, for the purposes of this book, I am going to take these concepts of the self-image and the limiting-image and show how they affect your ability as a public speaker. Obviously, the way you see yourself as a speaker will have a tremendous bearing on how you perform as speaker.

UNCOVERING HOW YOU SEE YOURSELF AS A SPEAKER

Even as you conduct your life within the limitations and exhilarations of your self-image, so you have a speaking-image that either helps you become more effective or limits you as a speaker. What kind of speaking-image have you built up out of your various speaking experiences? Have you fed your subconscious mind a string of poor evaluations of your speaking ability and created an image of mediocrity, or have you been building a strong and secure speaking-image as a result of responsive audiences?

It is necessary to uncover the status of your speaking-image, for you will speak in a way that is consistent with your image. If you see yourself as a boring speaker, you will be boring. If you see yourself as energetic, you will create energy. If you see yourself as stumbling through a manuscript, you will stumble. *You will act like the kind of speaker you think you are.*

The time has come for you to take a self-inventory to help you discover the kind of speaker you think you are. After this exercise is over, you will be asked to think about the kind of speaker you want to become; and, finally, you will be introduced to a series of mental activities that will help you become the kind of speaker you want to be.

TAKING A SELF-INVENTORY OF YOUR SPEAKING-IMAGE

1. Take a Seat in the Audience: Locate a place that is quiet and where you will not be interrupted. Sit down in a comfortable chair and for a few minutes simply concentrate on relaxing and letting the tension flow out of you. Now close your eyes and imagine that you are sitting in an audience that has come to hear you speak. See yourself looking at the empty podium and wondering what the speaker will be like.

Hear yourself being introduced and see yourself coming to the podium to speak. Observe the way you walk up there and note any mannerisms you might have. Hear your opening words. Think about how the sound of your voice comes across. See if there is eye contact with the audience and notice whether you have a habit of scratching your nose. Observe each and every detail you can within the realm of your imaginary evaluation.

Now open your eyes, and for the next twenty minutes write down your observations. Do it in an almost objective style: "The speaker was neat in his appearance. The speaker had a tendency to stare at the ceiling. The speaker seemed happy to be there. etc." Describe what you imagine to be the way you appear to others as a speaker.

This exercise can be extremely revealing. During a seminar on this subject, one participant blurted out:

"I didn't realize how dull I was. I was lying there with my eyes closed pretending to hear me speak; and would you believe it . . . I fell asleep!"

Another saw himself slowly shuffling up to the podium. He heard himself speaking in a low monotone and saw himself with his head buried in his notes. "It's hard for me to admit, but I never was aware before of how uninteresting I must appear to be."

One participant loved every minute of it: "I could listen to me speak all day! I had some great things to say and I said them well!"

On the other hand, let me warn you not to be discouraged if you didn't seem to come up with much in this exercise. We are not used to evaluating ourselves and certainly would have some problem getting outside ourselves and being objective.

The next test, though, will be the most revealing. For in the second part of this self-inventory you will be asked to get inside yourself as you appear as a speaker.

2. Get the Inside Story: Now begins the critical exercise of examining your speaker-image. Again, close your eyes, but this time imagine that you are on the platform getting ready to speak. The auditorium is packed, the time has come, you are introduced and you get up to go to the podium. Describe your feelings as you are walking up to the podium. Are you nervous, confident, excited, eager to start? Do you feel as if you are in charge of the situation or do you feel as if the roof is caving in?

Evaluate your delivery. Are you coming across as interesting, boring, enthusiastic, dull? Look at the audience. What do you see on their faces. Do they seem to be with you, uninterested, eager to hear? How does your body feel? Do you feel comfortable in your clothes? Are your gestures normal and natural or do you wish you could stick your hands in your pockets?

How many notes do you have in front of you and how much are you depending on them? Suppose a breeze should suddenly blow them away; what would be your reaction?

What happens when you finish speaking? Do you feel exhilarated, let-down, frustrated, satisfied? Do you feel as if you need an aspirin? What is the response of the audience? Do they applaud politely or do you hear words of appreciation and thunderous applause? Do they come by afterwards to talk with you? What are their comments?

As you leave the meeting, do you feel you never want to go through that experience again or do you feel that you can hardly wait for the next time?

Now open your eyes and begin to write down your impressions. Again, set them down as a series of statements: "As a speaker I see myself as . . ." Do this systematically beginning with your feelings after your introduction right through to the end.

What will begin to emerge will be a composite picture of the kind of speaker you think you are—your speaker's image. That is why it is important that you do the exercise as thoroughly and as honestly as possible. If you're not satisfied with the results the first time, give it a couple of days and try it again. Remember, what you are trying to uncover is the way you see yourself in your role as a speaker. This is not a test to see how good a speaker you are.

3. Locate Your Priorities: Now, from the results of these two exercises make two lists. The first is a list of what you consider to be your strong points in your speaking image. Again, frame the list in the terms: "As a speaker I am . . ." The second list you make should contain those areas where you feel you need to improve as a speaker. List them, but also list the improvement you would like to make. "As a speaker I am . . . I would like to be . . ." Note in definite terms the improvements you want to make because these will become your goals in the final exercises in this chapter on how to become the kind of speaker you want to be. At this point, we have simply helped you identify your problems. Later, you will be invited to use certain techniques to correct or change them.

Note that the whole intent of this book is to help you to discover Charis-magic power. That objective has not been lost in these exercises. In fact, the number one item in your list of priorities should be: "As a speaker I am . . . I would like to be Charis-magic—the kind of speaker who has the power to move people." This obviously is the number one goal, but we must frame it in our ability to have high expectancies and a growing speaking-image.

DEVELOPING A CHARIS-MAGIC EXPECTATION

I stated at the beginning of this chapter that one of the psychological conditions for the possibility of Charis-magic power is "Your own personal expectation of power." The persuasive speaker is marked by his expectation that powerful things will happen when he speaks. I showed how this expectation of power can be hindered by a limiting-image or a poor self-image, and, finally, I invited you to use a series of self-inventory techniques that would help you see how great your personal expectation is and how you see yourself as a speaker.

Now I want to concentrate on helping you become the kind of speaker you want to be—a Charis-magic speaker. This calls for stretching your expectations through a series of techniques I call *Creative Imagining.* To become a persuasive speaker, you begin by imagining how it would feel to already be one. You mentally play with the idea. You set before you the continuing picture of responsive crowds. You plant in your mind the image of being the kind of speaker who leaves them cheering.

Each day, for about half an hour, you prepare yourself mentally for power. You stretch your expectations to include the possibility of Charis-magic presentations.

CREATIVE IMAGINING—PRACTICE MAKES POSSIBLE

1. Feel the Warmth of Your Good Speaking Experiences: In a quiet and undisturbed atmosphere let your mind begin to remember those moments when you felt really alive and exhilarated as a public speaker. Think about the time when the crowd really broke up over a bit of your humor. Feel the flush of their warmth as you stand in the center of the laughter. Dwell on it. Enjoy it. Live it over and over again.

Think about the time you used an illustration that brought a hush over the room, that caught everyone up in the magic of the moment. Feel the atmosphere. See the look in everyone's eyes. Revel in the sense of power that came over you in that moment.

Think about a warm and responsive conclusion to one of your speeches. Hear the applause. Stretch it out. Let it continue to ring in your ears.

Dig deep into your memories, and every time you find a moment that made you feel alive and powerful as a speaker say to yourself:

"I've done it once. I can do it again!"

2. Deal With Your Disappointing Speaking Experiences: Think about those speaking experiences that have left you washed out and disappointed. Get them in front of you so you can face them and deal with them. Conclude in your mind that they were painful, but that you will not allow them to set the pattern of your expectations. Yes, they did happen, but they are not going to be the expected happening.

Think about that time when you blew the punch line to a story; but, so does everybody. Think about it, but don't dwell on it. Remember it, but when you do, apply what I call *the law of substitution.* Find another time when you told it right and the response was good, and think of that time as the norm.

Think about the time when you finished your speech to some polite and scattered applause, but challenge that experience. Apply the *law of substitution* and remember the time when the room was alive with appreciation and strong applause. Dwell on that experience as the more common one. Set the pattern. Whenever you have a disappointing speaking experience, challenge it, deal with it, substitute the memory of a stronger experience and "clean it out" of your speaking-image.

Some years ago, a man came to me because he had developed a very serious speaking problem. He was supposed to address a meeting of his peers and when he came to the podium he literally choked up. He couldn't get his words out and just stood there in silence looking into the eyes of a puzzled audience. Granted, this is a rare thing to have happen, but it did happen to him. Since then, he lived with a haunting fear that it might happen again. Every time he got ready to speak, the fear of that possibility swept through him. He came looking for help and I applied the *law of substitution.*

"Do you remember a time," I asked him, "when you went up to a podium to speak and you were flooded with feelings of warmth and appreciation?"

He thought for a long while. "Well, I don't know if this one counts, but a few years ago my Civic Club gave me an award for community service. They called me up to the podium to say a few words and would you believe that they actually stood up and cheered me every step of the way?"

"That's great! Did you enjoy it?"

"I loved it. It was one of the greatest things that ever happened to me."

"Okay, we've got what we need. Now this is what I want you to do. The next time you are sitting there waiting to be introduced to get up and make your speech, you start to remember the day you got your award. You imagine that it's happening right then and there and that the introducer is asking you to come to the podium to get your award; and when he announces your name, you go up there and say a few words."

He applied the technique and gradually it took its hold until it replaced his pattern of fear with a pattern of warmth.

3. Appeal to Future Speaking Experiences: At this level of developing your Charis-magic expectation, you let your mind go free. You see yourself as you want to be—the complete and power-filled speaker. You go beyond the limitations you see within your own personality and dare to believe that the possibility of Charis-magic power is yours.

Take this gradually at first. Don't try to force yourself to the point where you feel you are really deluding yourself; but gradually feed your mind with the expectation you desire. Tell yourself that there is no reason why you can't be a persuasive speaker. Make room for that possibility in your expectations.

Let the idea gradually work itself into your subconscious and your speaking-image; then, start your dress rehearsals. Prepare yourself for power by imagining instances of speaking that are all that you want them to be. Feed your subconscious mind your experiences by acting them out in your imagination. Hear the cheering crowd. See the tears in their eyes. Feel their warmth and anticipation. Tell a story and feel its impact. Make a telling point and sense the excitement of the audience.

Feed all the imaginary events into your mind and your mind will feed them into your subconscious data bank of speaking experiences.

Gradually, surely, inevitably, the changes in your speaking-image will bring changes in your speaking ability. Slowly, the transformation will take place as you act in a way that will be consistent with your growing assurance, as you become the kind of speaker you imagined yourself to be.

4. How To "Own The Crowd:" "Owning the crowd" is another technique that will help you develop a Charis-magic expectation of your audience. You view the audience as being "in your pocket"; they belong to you and you can do what you want with them.

If you see the audience as a threat, as distant from you and out to hurt you, they can be a real obstacle in your way to persuasive power. From the first moment you know you will be speaking to a group, until the last word of your actual speech, picture them in your mind as happy, receptive, warm and yours!

Always approach an audience having pre-conditioned yourself to feel that you are in charge. Imagine it and feel it beforehand. Practice it as a part of your daily ritual. Never walk onto a platform feeling that you are at the mercy of the audience around you. You might turn them into a lynch mob. "Own them," but treat them right. They deserve the best you have.

Key

THE STORY OF ONE MAN'S EXPECTATIONS

One of the most startling examples I have ever seen of Charis-magic expectation in action was in the life of a man in Central Florida who owned a variety of businesses and investments. He was shrewd, capable, respected and powerful, but he couldn't speak in front of an audience without stumbling over himself. He was naturally embarrassed and came to me for some personal help. In our conversation one day, I asked him if he ever went into a business deal expecting to be taken. I could tell that I startled him.

"I wouldn't go near a deal," he thundered, "if I didn't fully expect to win!"

"You mean if you went into a deal expecting to take a beating, it would make a difference?"

"You bet your life it would! If I went into a meeting with doubts, they would smell them a mile away and eat me alive. When you go for the kill in business, you've got to go expecting to win. You go in there half-hearted and expecting to lose and they'll carry you out."

"Well," I said, "If it works so well in business, why don't we make it work for you in your speaking?" His head snapped back. "Why don't we take that same winning expectation you have in your business life and carry it into the speaking arena? Right now you're letting them eat you alive. You have the needed drive. You know what it means to be a winner. We just have to get your expectation power tied to your speaking-image."

I asked him to set aside time every day, and I started him on a program of stretching his expectations and imagining his speaking success. I helped him see the crowds waiting to hear what a man of his stature had to say. I helped him see himself at the podium with the same confidence he had in business. I had him working day after day in creative imagining and mental practicing and slowly I noticed him start to change. It was gradual at first, but, always expecting, always imagining, he grew in confidence.

I added a few short speaking engagements. We took the strengths from each one and thought about them and enjoyed their warmth. We cast the weaknesses aside as incidental or buried them when we had to by using the *law of substitution*. I added some longer meetings. Now we concentrated on owning the crowd. Slowly he started to get through to them and move them, a little at first and then gaining momentum. I watched as he moved towards becoming the kind of speaker he wanted to be.

Then, one night it happened. At a political meeting in Orlando, Florida, I saw the final affirmation of his expectations—a radiant speaker, a powerful performance and a standing ovation.

None of it would have ever been possible if he hadn't seen it first in his imaginings. Before the fact, there had to be that magnificent expectation of Charis-magic power.

A SHORT WRAP-UP

In this chapter, I set out to deal with the first psychological condition for Charis-magic power in public speaking—the expectation of the speaker. I suggested that your own personal expectation of power is a necessary prerequisite for power to happen, and sought to share techniques of stretching your expectations. As I said, this is a necessary beginning, but it is only the opening of the door to Charis-magic power.

Now, you need to build on this expectation by coming to understand what has to take place between the speaker and the audience for this persuasive power to erupt. This will bring you to the second psychological condition of Charis-magic power mentioned at the opening of this chapter: "Your ability to build a relationship of trust with the audience." That will be taken up in the next chapter.

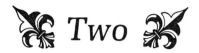 **Two**

Discovering the
Never-Fail Principle
of
Charis-Magic Power

Once you have prepared yourself personally for Charis-magic power by stretching your expectations, the next step is to start building a relationship of trust with your audience. This is the second psychological condition for persuasive power that I mentioned in the last chapter.

The kind of power you will have over your audience will be directly related to how strong a bond of trust you can establish. Where there is no trust, where there is only resistance, or at the best indifference, no real power is seen: but when trust binds the speaker and audience together, powerful events take place.

Basically, building trust is a selling job. It depends in large measure on your ability as a speaker to get through so-called audience resistance and "sell" yourself as the kind of person who can be trusted. In this chapter, we are going to take a hard look at these factors and leave you with several proven skills that will help you do your selling job in a natural and effective way.

SELLING YOURSELF FIRST

Every businessman knows the necessity of being able to build a trust relationship with his clients and customers, and I have spent a fair share of my professional career working with groups in developing this skill. The principle is both simple and powerful: the customer buys you before he buys your product or service. You have to sell yourself first!

The first time I heard this phrase, which now is bordering on becoming a cliché, I was at a real estate convention. There was an exhibitor who sold Beeper units. He was brash, energetic, a seasoned veteran in the selling business. I asked him about his work. He started slowly but gained momentum until, in a moment of towering pride, he exploded:

"They buy me! That's why they buy my Beeper. They buy me! These other guys have big names on their units—important names. Me ... I have a company no ones knows. You can't even see its name on the unit, it's so small. I don't want anyone to see it. They wouldn't know the company if they saw it. I sell my Beeper because my customers buy me! They trust me ... not the name on the product. Once they buy me, they just hand over their wallet and tell me to take what I want."

Certainly, if building trust is of importance in a business relationship, it is of no less importance in a speaking situation. In fact, in speaking, you are doing a selling job. The product may not be a can opener, but an idea, a viewpoint, a challenge. The principle is the same. First you sell yourself and then you sell the message.

When you sell, you sell in the market place. When you speak, you speak where there are people. The salesman has to know how to market his product. The speaker has to know how to market his message. The salesman can only make a sale if he gets through to the customer. The speaker can only experience Charis-magic power if he gets through to his audience.

HOW TO APPROACH YOUR AUDIENCE

Your audience presents an exciting challenge. The way you see them and your frame of mind in approaching them will determine the kind of challenge. Do you see them as obstacles to overcome or do you view them as good friends to enjoy? I have been amazed, over the years, to discover how many speakers would see their audiences as opponents who had to be beaten into submission. When I would ask why they used that approach, I'd get some kind of comment about audience resistance.

In fact, recently I heard an experienced speaker exhorting other speakers to go after this audience resistance in almost military terms:

"Remember, the audience is your enemy. You must be ready to beat your way through to victory. They will do everything they can to stop you. They will rattle you and distract you and give you an uneasy feeling that they might suddenly turn on you . . . but always remember, the winning speaker doesn't let it throw him. He plows on through all that resistance to ultimate victory."

You have my guarantee that if you view your audience in these terms you are headed for some rough water in your quest for persuasive power. Let me share some thoughts with you about handling resistance.

DON'T EXPECT "AUDIENCE RESISTANCE"

Your first lesson in dealing with your audience in order to build trust is "don't expect resistance!" Remember, you reflect your expectations in your actions. If you feel as if you are in the camp of the enemy, it will show through your speech, your nervous mannerisms, the very look in your eyes. Without being aware of it, you will unconsciously be generating the very conditions you are trying to avoid. If you come looking for the audience to give you a hard time, they probably will—at least in your own mind they will.

This is not just a trap for the beginning speaker. There have been times when I have fallen into the quicksand of poor audience expectation and ended up with a disappointing showing. I remember being called on to give the closing address at a convention in Miami. The minute I walked into the banquet hall, I just knew in my mind that I was headed for trouble. I found all kinds of things to complain about. The room was too large. The sound was poor. The tables were too far apart. The lighting was bad. The meal went on too long. But worst of all, the people weren't friendly. At least it seemed that way to me. I found every reason to be less than effective; and that night I bombed! With twenty years of speaking experience, I bombed! And I deserved to, because I came to that podium at odds with my audience.

People will usually give you back what you give them. They tend to echo your personality. If you come on warm and friendly, they will usually match you. If you come on as a threat, they will usually resist you. Granted, there are times when an audience is antagonistic, and rightly so. You may be supporting an unpopular position or negotiating a contract or bringing some bad news about company policy, and the resistance might be very real; but for now we are talking about our everyday garden-variety audience. How do you see them before you ever approach them? Do you see them in battle array or do you see them as warm, open and willing to hear what you have come to say?

Examine your audience-image. If you find that you are in conflict with the audience set out now to change that image. Using the techniques of Charis-magic expectations that I described in the first chapter, begin visualizing your audience as warm, friendly and receptive. See them as anxious to hear you and see yourself as "owning the crowd."

DISCOVERING THE TRUE SOURCE OF
AUDIENCE RESISTANCE

Advising you not to expect audience resistance does not mean that there is none. Resistance is present to some degree in every speaking situation, unless, of course, you are speaking to a familiar group who are all in sympathy with all you are saying. When revealed for what it really is, though, audience resistance can be dissipated like a mist by sunshine.

Resistance of this kind is not some special phenomenon that happens only in speaking situations. In simplest terms, it is the natural tension we feel whenever we meet a person for the first time. We have been conditioned from childhood to beware of strangers. Parents have warned us, "Don't talk to strangers, they can hurt you;" "Don't take gifts from strangers, they can harm you;" "Don't listen to strangers, they can lead you into danger." No wonder we feel a little apprehensive around a new person. Think of all the warnings you have received to walk carefully and keep your eyes open.

In a real sense, a speaking situation is a large scale encounter of a stranger meeting strangers. No wonder you sense some kind of tension in the air and vague, uneasy feelings of some kind of threat. For the most part, the audience doesn't know you and you don't know them. Both of you are naturally a little cautious about each other and wondering what to expect from each other.

This tension, the tension that naturally arises when stranger meets stranger, is primarily the source of what has been called audience resistance. To handle it and deal with it as a speaker you will need to give the audience certain assurances of the kind of person you are. You must set in motion certain "vibes" that will say to the audience, "Relax, I have not come to harm you." In fact, all of Chapter Four in this book deals with this one issue—"How to present yourself to an audience as friendly and non-threatening." The point I have tried to make to you in this chapter is that, in like manner, you should see the audience as friendly and non-threatening. Who wants to build a trust relationship with an audience if there is a haunting fear that if they get close to us they are going to kill us?

REACHING OUT TO THE AUDIENCE

This book does not deal with the many psychological facets of the problem of trusting other people; but it is a telling point that if you are to build a relationship of trust with your audience you will need to expose part of yourself in an open and almost defenseless way. This may not be easy. You may have to deal with a fear of personal rejection; but the attempt has to be made.

This is not anything new to a speaker. In a real sense you cannot speak without being exposed. You are vulnerable. In a unique fashion you stand up there and make statements about yourself, your feelings, your beliefs, your product. Sometimes this can prove to be especially frightening. There is nowhere to hide, unless of course you bury yourself in some other personality.

Let us come back to the point at hand. You cannot expect your audience to let their defenses down and open themselves to you and your words unless you make the first move. You must sell yourself as the kind of person who can be trusted; but to sell yourself you must be yourself!

TO SELL YOURSELF — BE YOURSELF

Many a speaker trying to reach for Charis-magic power in his presentations has unwittingly stripped himself of his most powerful tool of persuasion by trying to imitate some other speaker. I don't have to tell you how hard it is to listen to a speaker who is acting like someone else. You want to be confronted by real flesh and blood. You want to feel that the speaker is giving you a piece of himself and not some poor imitation. The actor-speaker always loses credibility from the very first word; and because you don't buy him as genuine, you don't buy his message.

A friend of mine, Win Pendleton, a thoroughly enjoyable humorous speaker with a half dozen books on the subject, places great stress on the importance of being yourself. For him it is one of the cardinal rules of public speaking.

Win likes to illustrate the value of projecting your own image by telling the story of the rising young nightclub comic. The comic was struggling through his act one night and getting very few laughs when Jack Benny and some of his friends entered the lounge. Seeing an opportunity to impress one of the great names in show business, the young man abandoned his rehearsed routine and started imitating Jack Benny. When the show was over he rushed up to Benny and asked him, "How did you like the imitation I did of you?"

"Well," Benny replied, "after watching you, all I can say is, one of us is lousy!"

Win shared with me how this principle was brought home to him personally. In his early years he was taking private lessons from a speech expert. One night he was urged to watch a television show where Charles Laughton, the great character actor, read excerpts from the classics of literature including Lincoln's Gettysburg Address.

The next day when he went to class, his instructor handed him a copy of Lincoln's famous speech and asked him to read it. Trying to impress his teacher he stood, posed dramatically, and started to orate à la Laughton. He was hardly finished before his instructor came flying out of his seat shouting, "No .. no . . . no! That's terrible, Win! I didn't ask you to read it like Laughton, I asked you to read it—you! Don't you ever forget, it's better to be a first-rate Win Pendleton than a second-rate Charles Laughton!"

Many times I've heard someone say, "If I could only speak like you, I'd be thrilled." On the surface it sounds like a real compliment, and I usually take it that way. In the light of reality, though, I can't kid myself. I can speak the way I do because it is consistent with my total personality, not because I have discovered some "disembodied technique." My style might be completely wrong for someone else and even make them come off looking like a phony. That is why I don't get concerned about other people using my material. They may have my words, but they don't have "the way I say my words" as a total personality. I've even had people come to me and tell me, "You know, I heard you tell a story at a convention last year; and I loved it. In fact, I used it the very next week in one of my speeches . . . and it fell flat on its face. I guess it wasn't all I thought it was cracked up to be."

Stevie Wonder has an album out called *Songs In The Key of Life.* If I had just one to give a speaker I would call it the *Key of B Natural.* I can't stress its importance enough. When you appear on that platform, the impression you need to make is "what you see is what you get!"

WORKING AT BEING YOURSELF

I knew a businessman who was also an effective speaker in his own right. He was in his middle fifties, the president of a large manufacturing firm in Massachusetts. We were having dinner together and talking about different platform personalitites and how they generated power in their speeches. I started to make some suggestions to him about changing his own style, telling him how I would do it and that maybe he should adopt my style. In the middle of my comments he interrupted me, smiled gently and said:

"You know, I'd get bored sick if I had to see a hundred Dick Milhams running around the platforms all over the country. You are unique, but only because you are you—one of a kind. But it would wear thin if everyone had your style.

Milham, a lot of your power is in the fact that you are what you are, both on and off the stage. It would never work for me. I am what I am; and to tell you the truth, I'd be downright uncomfortable being a sample of your style. Just help me become more of what I am and help me find better ways to get that across to my audience."

Powerful advice!

I want to introduce you to several exercises to help you become "more of what you are" and, in doing so, help you build your trust relationship with your audience.

1. Finding Your Level of Consistency: Are you basically the same person on the platform as you are off; or are you a different person when you get up to speak? I have seen quiet personalities who suddenly burst forth like a string of firecrackers being lit. They exploded all over the place for a short time, but when it was all over, only the smoke remained. Others who otherwise are alive and animated get up to speak and you feel as if you are going to have to pry every other word out of their mouths.

I remember, some years ago, being invited to keynote the meeting of a national sports association. Before the session started, I enjoyed speaking to a young minister who was to give the invocation. He was warm and cordial, and I immediately liked him as a person. I noticed, as any speaker would, that his voice was rather soft and slightly high-pitched, but certainly easy to listen to.

The time came for his prayer. I bowed my head and was suddenly broadsided by a booming voice proclaiming thunderously, "Oh, Lord, we have come into Thy presence . . ." I popped my head up out of curiosity to see if they had slipped in some ringer for the prayer, but no, there he was . . . talk about changes on the podium!

A speech should flow naturally out of your personality. There should be a continuity between the man you are as a speaker and the man you are around your friends.

Video-Tape Yourself: One of the most revealing experiences that can happen to you is to sit back and see yourself as you appear to others. In the first chapter, I asked you to try it in your imagination, but now I am suggesting that you actually see it.

The best way to get the most out of this exercise is to have yourself taped during one of your actual speeches. You might consider contacting the Communications Department of a local college and see if you can get some students to do the taping as a project, at your expense. If this is impractical, then consider going to a local studio, renting, or borrowing the equipment. You might even consider having a video-cassette made so you can play and replay it within the privacy of your own home.

Do whatever you have to do to get the chance of seeing yourself as you appear to others. This is not too much to ask if the end result helps to produce the power you are looking for.

In viewing yourself you can get bogged down in a lot of personal criticisms; but the point of this exercise is to ask one simple question: Is what you see and hear consistent with the kind of person you are off the platform? Make notes whenever you notice a mannerism, gesture, quirk of speaking that makes you feel and seem unnatural or artificial. Ask yourself where you picked it up. Are you subconsciously imitating another speaker along the way who has made an impact on you?

I don't mean to say that you can't learn a tremendous amount from other speakers. We all have incorporated elements of others in our style, but those elements should enhance and be consistent with our total personality, not detract from it.

Relish what you like about what you see, but expose what is hurting your integrity as a consistent personality.

Make a Television Appearance: Many people have had their public profile shaken by an appearance on television. Take advantage of every opportunity that might come your way to appear on this medium. It could be an appearance on a local talk show, a news interview, a guest shot on a public service program, or even your own business commercials.

Tape All Your Speeches: Listen and ask yourself how you feel you are coming across. Do you sense a distance in your voice or do you feel as if "he's talking right at me!" A word of caution; the first few times you really concentrate on listening to yourself might be a little unnerving. This is natural. We are not used to hearing ourselves speak, especially not as some disembodied voice coming out of nowhere.

In listening, try to identify those features that seem inconsistent with your everyday speaking voice. For instance, you might note that your pitch is slightly higher than normal. This is usually a result of the tightening of your vocal cords caused by nervous tension. As you learn to relax on the podium, this will disappear.

You might observe that your pace is faster as a result of this nervous tension, or your diction is overdone in an attempt to be too precise. You might even have one of your speeches transcribed to paper and just sit down and look at the vocabulary you used. Ask if it is consistent with your usual way of speaking or have you suddenly "put on airs?"

Take a Friend With You to Your Next Meeting: After all,

who is better qualified to know what you are like in your day-to-day personality. Ask him to become a part of the audience and to evaluate how naturally you seemed to come across. Let him tell you if he felt he was looking at a stranger or was listening to his "good old buddy."

Be cautious about some friends. Sometimes they wouldn't hurt you for the world. They would rather cut the truth a little than give it to you straight. Before you begin let your friend know that you are not looking for his compliments but for his help. Also remember that he is not a qualified speech critic. All you want is for him to serve as a barometer of how well you are adjusting your personality to the speaking situation.

2. How To Be Natural In Your Delivery: Another technique of learning to be yourself in order to sell yourself involves helping you deliver your material to your audience in a warm and natural way. This technique depends on your ability to imagine that you are speaking to a single person and not to a whole audience.

An audience has no tangible existence. It is made up of individual people, though, who *do* have. This is the reason for that classic bit of advice given to every fledgling speaker: "Pick out someone in the audience and deliver your speech just to him. Imagine that he's the only one out there and talk to him one on one."

I want to refine this exercise for you in two ways. *First*, I want to suggest that you think of delivering your speech not to just anyone in the audience, but to someone who is very special to you. Choose someone who means a lot and brings out the genuine warmth in you. Speak to *that* person and you will slowly begin to transform your speaking-image to one consistent with your personal-image.

Second, prepare for your speeches by mentally projecting this person in front of you. Notice the subtle changes that take place as you practice; the softening of your language or the interjection of personal remarks. Feel how the quality of your material begins to improve and how your illustrations seem to become more alive.

This is a powerful mental tool. You can manipulate your

power in a dozen different ways by utilizing it. For instance, suppose you were delivering your speech to a hundred tough-minded steel workers. Lay that image in front of you in your mental preparation and you will see some radical changes in your vocabulary, illustrations and tone quality. Note, that I am not saying that we should stop coming on as friendly and natural. What I am saying is that by utilizing this tool we can tune in to the temperment of the audience and find the best way to relate to them.

Sadly, this tool has been used as a destructive force. Many times a speaker has held before his mind and wrapped in hate the image of a person he wants to destroy. He waves that image like a red flag in his mind to arouse his fury until it spills over in vehement outbursts to his audience.

On the other hand, this tool of creative imagining can help you overcome any lingering problem you might have with audience resistance. Several years ago I introduced this technique in a seminar I was leading in Public Speaking. Just as I did with you, I asked each member in the class to come up with someone he could put in front of him to help him relate to the audience. One lovely lady came up to me and asked, "Would it be all right if I talk to my basset hound? He's the only one who ever listens to me."

I'd heard them all, but that one sure topped them. I couldn't help laughing, but then I started thinking; she had found her key for her mental preparation, and a powerful one at that. Could there be anything that would make you feel more welcome or warm you up any more than looking out at your audience and seeing a big, lovable, floppy-eared basset hound sitting on a seat in the front row? And, if you really want to let your imagination go wild, and come close to rolling on the floor with laughter, imagine a whole auditorium full of basset hounds! In my book that sure beats imagining everyone sitting around in underwear.

3. Doing What Comes Naturally: People warm up to you when you act natural. Sometimes it can happen through a small gesture—some act that simply says, "Here I am, and this is the kind of person I am." It might be something as simple as loosening your tie, or admitting you lost your way to the auditorium.

Each year I'm usually invited as a Commencement speaker at a college somewhere. I'm always excited. Graduating is a special event filled with all kinds of human emotions. I love the occasion, but, in all honesty, I always used to feel a little cramped by the barrage of formality that goes with it. Inevitably, I am robed with the mark of my degrees and fitted with a mortarboard on my head.

On one particular night, the hall was packed with over three thousand graduates and their families. The preliminaries were long and my introduction was longer. And now it was time for me to speak. I walked to the platform, stood in silence for a long moment and then reached up, took off my cap, and placed it on the podium. "I hope you don't mind," I said. I brushed back my hair and made a few comments about how I never could wear those caps too gracefully. It was a simple act—nothing dramatic, but a gesture that said, "I just want to be myself with you."

I followed by saying, "Thank you for letting me get a little comfortable. I'm here because I want to share some thoughts with you, friend to friend. This is your graduation, so if you don't mind I'd like to direct my thoughts to you. If the others here want to listen in that's fine; but I've come because I have something special to say to you."

The concluding standing ovation lingers in my mind; but more than that, the key I found, the key of trying to be myself, has been used on many other occasions.

RESPECTING YOUR AUDIENCE

During the course of this chapter you have been given a series of mental and practical exercises to help you meet audience resistance and sell yourself as the kind of person who can be trusted. These skills are not attempts to manipulate the audience but are meant to put them at ease with you and make them more receptive to hearing your message.

I have tried to assist you in seeing the audience in different ways—as friendly, as warm, as receptive—and now I want you to look at them as worthy of your respect. *Audiences warm up to speakers who treat them with respect.* Everyone wants to be recognized for who he is and wants to be treated like a human being. Audiences also have a right to expect that when you approach them you are not looking to manipulate them. One speaker's comment about an audience he was about to address still rings in my ears: ". . . they are just like chickens ready to be plucked!"

Respect for your audience will make a difference in your preparation and your materials. Your audience deserves your best. They are giving up a piece of their lives in exchange for whatever you have come to bring them. Respect for them should result in a message that is worthwhile. This is a profound responsibility. Public speaking is fun, it's exhilarating, and it's challenging, but above all . . . it is an invitation to walk into another person's life and have your say.

A Story With a Sting: The memory of when I learned this lesson of respecting an audience is still alive in my mind. I was scheduled to be the keynote speaker at the state convention of the Florida Hotel and Motel Association in Boca Raton. I arrived early and was meeting some of the over three hundred registrants, managers, sales managers and the like of the major hotels and motels throughout the state.

I had worked my way around to a banquet table in the farthest corner of the room and approached one of the men seated there. I put on a smile, held out my hand and said, "Hello, I'm Dick Milham from Orlando, Florida. I'm your speaker for tonight." He took my hand, looked me squarely in the eyes and said:

"What kind of b_____s_____ can I expect from you?"

My first reaction was anger. I felt that he had no right, especially as a stranger, to attack me like that; but as I walked away, I started to think about it. You know, he had every right to ask me what I was going to do with the time he was going to give me—the minutes that he would never live again.

I had to ask myself what I was going to give him in exchange for those minutes—a message that would reach him, or more hot air?

He is now a part of my mental preparation. Whenever I am preparing for a new engagement, I put him up there in front of me and all of my materials, illustrations, humor, must pass the test of his haunting words.

POINTS TO REMEMBER:

1. First sell yourself and then you can sell your message.
2. In dealing with audience resistance don't expect resistance.
3. Audience resistance is the natural tension you feel when you meet a stranger.
4. To sell yourself, be yourself.
5. Work at finding the consistency between the man you are on the platform and the man you are off the platform.
6. Prepare for speaking to your audience by seeing them as individuals.
7. Respect your audience as deserving the best you have to give.

From the speaker's viewpoint, Charis-magic power depends on your own expectation of power and your ability to build a relationship of trust with your audience. In order to build this trust, though, you have to give the audience certain assurances of the kind of person you are. These assurances or "vibes" or "ingredients in the magic potion of power" will be revealed in the next chapter. Up to this point you have said "trust me," but now the audience wants you to give them some reasons why they should. They want you to convince them that you are the kind of person they can trust. Once this selling job has been done. Charis-magic power is on the way.

Three

Five "Assurances" That Guarantee Charis-Magic Results

DEALING WITH A WARY PUBLIC

In this process of building trust with your audience you will need to sell yourself as the kind of person who can be trusted. This seems simple enough until you realize that you are going to be dealing with people who are being warned every day to "watch out for hustlers."

Any day of the week you can pick up your newspaper and read about some "poor sucker" who was cleaned out in a fraud game, or about the "sweet little old lady" who bought worthless stock, or about a "miracle drug" that turned out to be shredded hay.

When the public looks for some kind of answer and protection from all this they are told: "Caveat emptor—let the buyer beware that he is buying at his own risk!" What this amounts to is that Mr. John Q. Public is being told that the responsibility for protecting himself against being cheated falls squarely on his own shoulders.

He is being warned to "read the fine print," "look out for loopholes," "check with the Better Business Bureau," "look out for con artists," and "don't trust anyone who rolls up to your house with a truck loaded with tar and gravel and wants to fix your roof."

No one wants to feel cheated and many frustrated people have tried to strike back. Driving through a small town in northern Georgia I saw a truck stopped at an intersection. It was painted bright yellow and scrawled across the doors and side panels in red letters was this message: "Look at the lemon I bought!" Appropriately, he had also scratched in the name of the local dealer.

People are being disappointed with warranties that are worthless, safety features that are dangerous, and poor service that is still expected to get a tip. All around us are flashing signs warning, "Look before you leap!"

The speaker who ignores this kind of negative conditioning in the public, or pretends he doesn't have any skeptics in his audience, is headed for serious trouble in trying to build his trust relationship. A Pollyanna attitude will not get through to a public that is saying more and more, "Show me!"

The public needs assurances from you before they will trust you. They need to feel that, despite everything else, they have met someone they can really believe. This is a selling job! It depends on your ability to gather your audience into a "zone of trust."

BUILDING A "TRUST ZONE"

In the study of people dynamics much is said about the "comfort zone." This is a relationship and situation where a person feels safe and comfortable. Much is made of the tension and anxiety that comes when a person is forced to explore new territories and different activities. This theory of the "comfort zone" is also used to explain why there is resistance to change of any kind; and why it is difficult to get some salespersons to do prospecting "out there in the jungle." The familiar feels comfortable and safe; the unfamiliar feels uncomfortable and threatening.

A persuasive speaker builds a "trust zone." This is a psychological situation much like the "comfort zone" where people in the audience feel at ease around you and are receptive to your message. If for any reason, though, they remain outside the "trust zone" they will feel uncomfortable and you will have a difficult time reaching them with your message.

This "trust zone" is built out of five assurances that the speaker gives about himself—assurances that generate the climate where Charis-magic power flourishes!

FIVE ASSURANCES THAT GUARANTEE POWER

Convincing the audience that you are a speaker who can be trusted relies on generating five assurances about yourself. Your audience needs to feel that:

- you are *friendly* and not a threat
- you *know* what you are talking about
- you are *sincere* and can be believed
- you *care* about each one personally
- you *have* a message that will *benefit* each one

These five assurances that you are *friendly, knowledgeable, sincere, caring* and have a *beneficial message* are the very heart of Charis-magic power—the power to move people!

This is not an arbitrary list pulled out of the air. Every assurance has been carefully distilled from the very best in psychological research and personal experience. They are—each and every one—necessary ingredients in the "potion of Charis-magic power." To be effective, though, it is critical that you use them in the right proportions. Each assurance has a degree of power on its own; but together and under the right circumstances, they generate great power—Charis-magic power.

THE LAW OF SYNERGISM

In geometry you probably learned that "the whole is equal to the sum of its parts." In chemistry there is another law, the law of synergism that states: "the whole is greater than its parts" . . . or better yet, "the effect of the parts together is greater than their effect each alone." Two chemicals that are innocuous can do powerful things when they get together.

This synergism is the secret of these assurances. Each one standing alone has some effect, but when they are brought together they produce Charis-magic power. Alone, their effect can be reduced like that of a single violin string. That one string is limited in its scope and range of effects; but when all the strings on the violin are used, they produce a symphony of sound.

Some problems arise in public speaking from the "one-string player," the speaker who latches on to just one of these assurances and beats it into the ground. The result is what I have come to call the backlash effect.

A PORTFOLIO OF ONE-STRING PLAYERS

Charis-magic power comes from the synergistic effect of bringing the five assurances together. When a speaker elevates just one of these assurances to his central theme, he doesn't create power, but rather weakness. This is what I call the backlash effect. Elevating just one assurance to the exclusion of the others is like playing on one violin string. Eventually it gets boring, and if you listen long enough, it will start to sound ridiculous. Over the years I have met and categorized "one-string players." If for nothing more than the sheer fun of it, I'd like you to meet them:

The Gusher: trying so hard to appear friendly, this type is a back-slapping, joke-telling, running torrent of comments like: "... so good to be here," "I love every one of you!" "I have never been so excited!" Everybody's a friend, and everything is "fantastic" and the whole world is a bowl full of cherries ... Sometimes, you feel you would just like to stand up and yell out to this type, "For God's sake ... please quit smiling! I don't think I can take any more ..."

The Egg Head: he *knows* he should let the audience know that he knows; but for him it becomes almost an obsession . . . always quoting some source . . . always referring to some authority . . . always citing page and chapter . . . You start to feel as if you are listening to a walking encyclopedia. He thinks he sounds as if he knows it all, but he translates to "boring at best." You feel like telling him to go and thumb through his books on someone else's time!

The Boy Scout: "a scout is trustworthy . . ." and this speaker doesn't let you forget it! He sounds as if he's signing off a letter every few minutes with his "Sincerely yours." He is always assuring you that he is "sincerely interested" in every little thing . . . in fact he is so sincere I'm beginning to get the feeling that he's sincerely insincere . . . sincerely!

The Bleeding Heart: this speaker really *cares* and you can measure how much by the number of sobs and little catches in his throat when he gets "all choked up!" The emotion flows like a river and you feel as if you'd better stand up in your seat before you get drowned by the flood of tears gushing down from the podium . . . the thing that bothers you, though, is the uneasy feeling that if you took a good, close look into those tears . . . you'd see crocodiles swimming around.

The Hustler: has he got a deal for you! . . . all kinds of benefits and grand prizes . . . but you just know that nobody gives away something for nothing . . . you know there's got to be a hook in it somewhere . . . if you believed everything this guy is offering . . . you'd be lighting cigars with hundred dollar bills . . . "Hey, fellow . . . pack up your sidewalk suitcase and move on! There may be a sucker born every minute . . . but you just lost this pigeon!"

Certainly there aren't any pure "one string players" around but the message is simple: be careful how many times you "go to the well"; you might come up empty.

BALANCING YOUR ASSURANCES

My warning about "one-string players" does not mean that every speech uses these assurances to the same degree. Obviously, the *purpose* of your speech will dictate to a large measure which of these assurances comes into play.

If you are speaking to a Rotary Club on the problem of nuclear waste, you will certainly need to set in motion solid knowledgeable vibes—"I have spent the last twenty years of my life studying this problem . . ." Because of the nature of the issue you might also show a strong note of caring—"I am concerned about our water and air. . . ." and benefit—"We need to get this problem under control so we can assure that your health and that of your family will be protected."

If you are a policeman and you have been invited to speak to a class of ninth graders on "It Won't Be Long Until You Are Driving," you certainly need to establish that you are friendly—"I remember the first time I drove a car . . .it was a beat up old hunk of nuts and bolts and I thought it would fall apart right under me . . ." and you care—"I have two teenagers at home and I worry about them every time they borrow my keys . . ." and benefit—"I'm talking about saving your life . . ."

Suppose you are participating in a membership drive of your local Chamber of Commerce. When approaching other business people you certainly will be getting the vibe of sincerity out front . . .—"I really believe in this organization . . . I've been a member ever since I moved to the area . . ." and benefit—"I can't tell you how many times my membership has been the key to bringing me new business . . ."

If you are presenting the Annual Report at a meeting of your stockholders, you certainly will be knowledgeable—"You will notice that in the column on assets . . ." but this also would be an excellent opportunity to send off some friendly vibes—"I have looked forward for a long time to meeting many of you personally . . ." and benefits—"This report will make you feel very good about your investment in this company . . ."

Friendly, knowledgeable, sincere, caring, a message with a benefit: all these assurances can help you produce Charis-magic power in your presentations when used in balance with one another. In the chapters that follow you will be invited to take a look at each of these in detail and will be given methods of building them into your speech; but first let me give you an exercise to help you find out how well you are doing your "balancing act."

TESTING FOR BALANCE

I want to invite you to examine your speech material to discover which of these assurances are in the spotlight, in the wings, or not on stage at all. The most graphic approach is to have one of your taped speeches transcribed to paper. Take a red felt-tip pen and go over every sentence, every illustration, every new thought and stroke over it with F (friendly), K (knowledgeable), S (sincere), C (caring), or B (benefit). There may be some instances when you are not sure which letter to put down—"I feel that if we get this twenty percent increase in taxes as I predict (K) we are all going to suffer; and that bothers me (C)!"—put them both down.

When you have finished, run a quick total and see how the assurances stack up. Remember, though, to take into consideration the purpose of your speech. For instance, if its prime purpose was to inform a group of a new product, you certainly will be ranking K high on the list with a lot of red strokes.

Note what assurances are conspicuous by their absence and ask yourself why they didn't make the scene. Was it because of intentional design, or the fact that you felt a little uncomfortable with them or "just the way the cookie crumbles."

Friendly, sincere, caring are all assurances that primarily show up as the result of your sharing a piece of yourself on a very human level. Sometimes this proves very difficult for some people. You will need to come to grips with whether you feel comfortable whenever you are called on to share yourself or whether you find it easier to hide behind the K's and the B's. This is not meant to be an indictment of any kind. We all must perform within the framework of our personalities if we are to be believed; but if it is a fact that "personal revelations" are a problem, you need to confront it honestly and decide how to handle it. I hope the remainder of this book will give you some guidelines and direction.

Another means of checking your assurances level is to work directly with a tape recording of one of your speeches. Take a piece of paper and write Purpose across the top. Then down the side, with plenty of space between, write the letters F, K, S, C, or B. Turn the recorder on and begin your analysis. Whenever you hear an assurance, give yourself a red check by the letter, and, if at all possible, make a note or write a key word that will remind you what the thought was.

This is an excellent technique to use whenever you have the opportunity to hear another speaker. Keep some index cards in your pocket and simply pull one out, write the title of the speech across the top, put the letters down the side and begin checking them as you listen to the speech. At the end, you will be amazed to discover how the assurances he gave either supported the purpose of his speech or left it hanging out in left field somewhere. I have done this time and time again and discovered a strong correlation between a man's power to move his audience and his utilization of assurances.

PUTTING THE TEST TO WORK

I used this technique several years ago to clear up a mystery. I was called by the Executive Director of an organization responsible for raising funds much like United Way, Fair Share and the like. Because he was having trouble raising the budget for that year, he had taken to the speaking circuit to "tell the story." He felt that he was ineffective in his presentation and wanted me to give him some direction on how to improve his speeches.

I attended his next speaking engagement at a local women's club. Taking out an index card, I listed the assurances down the side (friendly, knowledgeable, sincere, caring, benefits) and wrote the word Purpose across the top. As he spoke, I did my analysis, checking off the assurances as they came out of his speech. When he finished, my card was loaded with F's (friendly) and K's (knowledgeable) but only showed a few scattered S's (sincere), C's (caring) and B's (benefits).

Later we sat down together and talked about the results. I asked him about his purpose in speaking to the ladies:

"Well, I guess I wanted to get people to support this campaign and come across with some money."

I looked down at my card at the word Purpose and

noticed that I had put a large question mark after it. I said, "To be very honest, Bill, you didn't come across that way to me, and I think I can show you why."

I took out the index card and showed him my analysis and explained it. "Bill, what all these F's and K's mean is that as a speaker you come across like a nice guy who knows a lot about his subject. There is no question in my mind that you are likeable; and your speech was loaded with statistics and facts, all the way from the number of migrant workers and unemployed in the area to data on teenage pregnancies and child abuse. You sure convinced me you knew what you were talking about."

"The problem, though," I said, pointing to the other assurances, "is that I didn't feel any sense of your own personal involvement. I didn't get the impression that all this really mattered to you. Let me ask some honest questions, and I hope you don't mind. Do you really care about your work?"

"Certainly I do! It means a lot to me."

"Okay, are you really sincere in your desire to raise these funds and help people?"

"Of course I am! I couldn't do this work if I didn't feel that way. It's certainly not the salary."

"Tell me, will raising these funds and helping people benefit this community in any way?"

"In a dozen different ways!"

"Well, Bill, I didn't hear any of them. I just heard someone who wanted to get into my pocket for some reason. I really didn't know what difference it would make to me personally.

"Bill, you came across with a lot of facts, but you didn't convince me that I should support "your cause." In fact, that might be the key to explain what I mean. You came across as a speaker who wanted me to support a cause. I didn't feel the impact of your cause.

"Now Bill, I know your work in the office has become primarily administrative, hasn't it?" He nodded affirmatively. "Well, I can appreciate the problem of pulling you out of that world of nuts and bolts and slapping you in front of an audience. I know I might be sounding rough on you, but I'm glad you asked me to work with you. Now let's get down to it."

I helped him rework his speech content, unloading a lot

of dry statistics (K) and injecting personal notes like, "It means a lot to me to be in this job and I want to serve you in the best way possible. "(C)" and "Sometimes I get a little tired in my work, as all of us do, but then I see it for what it is—a chance to help people and serve my community." (S)

I talked to him about showing the benefits of the campaign in concrete, individual illustrations. So he added material like the story of a teenager who was headed for jail but instead was put into a work program by one of the organizations. "That one incident saved you, the tax payers in this country, thousands of dollars."

He told about the drug education program in the Junior High School, ". . . to help your young people," and he told about an old couple on social security who were helped to keep their lives together because of a Meals on Wheels program; ". . . they are holding up their heads and trying to contribute rather than ending up in a county home at your expense."

I told him how to end his speech by asking for some action from his audience. "You can't just let them sit there on their wallets. Give them a plan of action, a pledge card to sign or a number to call, or get their business cards and follow up . . . but do something to get them personally involved!"

He called a few months later to tell me how his speaking had shown much improvement, but most of all, how the campaign had shown such dramatic results. "Best of all," he concluded, "my life has taken on so much more vitality since I started to share my work with others from the platform."

The key to Charis-magic power is synergism, the balanced blending of assurances (friendly, knowledgeable, sincere, caring and benefits) to produce an effect that is greater than the parts. As you remember in the introduction to this book, I defined *magic* as "the power to produce *effects* that seem more than human." That's synergism—that's Charis-magic!

HOW TO PREPARE YOUR AUDIENCE
TO EXPECT YOU

In the pages that follow I have set aside a chapter for each of these assurances and in them offer you skills on how to use them in your speech content and delivery, but before that, a final matter that deserves attention.

What a great feeling, to approach your audience ready to get down to it! You've worked hard. You're coming with high expectations. Your material is brimming with exciting possibilities of Charis-magic action. You can hardly wait to begin. The introduction is concluded. You move confidently to the podium. The words begin to flow from your lips, and . . . nothing happens!

The people just seem to sit there looking at you, unresponsive and almost disinterested. They seem to be in a fog or at best just plain tired. I know the feeling!

I keenly recall a situation at a banquet. I got up and started out with my best shots . . . and nothing! My humor just seemed to lie there and groan . . . my words seemed to roll out of my mouth and hit the floor. If ever I had a sense of panic, I was feeling it then.

I've since analyzed that situation and others like it, and have found in all of them that, although I was prepared as a speaker, *the audience wasn't prepared to hear me!* They didn't have the slightest idea of who I was, what I was doing there, or what I had come to say. Here is the lesson to learn: *where there is no audience expectation, there will be very little audience reaction!* I've learned from hard experience that I am headed for trouble when the man who is going to introduce me comes up to me and asks, "What are you going to talk about?"

Some of the hardest meetings I have ever prepared for are those where I have been asked to "just come and talk on something." An audience, like the speaker, must have some expectations. If you have to round up the audience mentally and spend the first half of your speech justifying your right to be there and convincing them that you have a right to be heard, you will have more of a problem than you should in building your "trust zone."

I titled this section "How To Prepare Your Audience To Expect You." In some ways this is misleading. In the majority of situations, you have to depend on those who invited you to prepare the audience for your coming; but at least here are some guidelines that should be helpful to you.

Ask What Is Expected of You: When you are invited to

speak, ask very candidly what they expect from you. Are they looking for a comedian or some one to explain something, or a motivation speaker? Find out what is going on in their minds and what precipitated the invitation. Obviously, something was said about finding a speaker and your name came up. If they are just trying to fill out their calendar for the month, make them say so. There's no way you are going to really satisfy an audience if you don't know what they are expecting you to do.

If they themselves don't know, then explore some subjects with them. Ask them if they would like to hear a speech on "The Secret of Making Money" ("No . . . we heard that one last week!") or "The Wonder of Polliwogs." ("Not interested.") Keep at it until you come up with something; just don't let them leave you floundering on your own. Make them assume the responsibility for the subject by agreeing that it would be appropriate for the situation. Then you can assume responsibility for the content. It's easy for someone to invite you and then, when you don't "ring the bell," wash his hands of you and make you the heavy. Ask what is expected!

In my own work I have been fortunate to work with some exceptionally fine meeting planners who practice this secret religiously. They do everything possible to tune the speaker in to the needs of the audience. I've had them travel over two thousand miles and spend several days with me just helping me prepare to be the best for them and their meeting. That's when I'm at my best and my audiences get their money's worth.

My first question of these meeting planners is always the same: "What do you expect me to do? In what way can I be of service with my skills?" Granted, your speeches may be limited in scope, but that's all right. Just be sure they know what you are coming to say and that they agree it will be appropriate.

Settle on A Title For Your Presentation: Find a title that isn't just "cute" at best or misleading at worst. Your title should accurately indicate the content of your speech in an interesting way. "Hot Spots In the Old Sky Tonight" is cute but it doesn't say anything about the speech. You might want to try, "The Functions of Solar Energy," but who wants to listen to that? Settle for something like, "The Fascinating World of Solar Energy," and then plan to make it that way. More about titles and how to prepare them in a later chapter.

Advertise Your Subject: Give your audience a chance to decide whether they want to hear you or not. Ask that your subject be announced in advance if at all possible, or published in their weekly newspaper, or sent out in a mailing. Some people might not have the slightest bit of interest in your subject. Don't take it personally. Granted, this might bruise your ego, but it is better that they don't come than have them slip out and tell you later, "I had a bad cough and I didn't want to disturb the meeting."

Deliver What You Advertise: An audience can feel deceived and misled if you pull the old "bait and switch" on them with your subject. I still get angry when I remember an incident that happened to me several years ago. I got up early in the morning after just a few hours sleep to attend a breakfast meeting to hear the subject, "How To Live Longer." The speaker was an authority from a large and famous medical center. I was interested in the subject and went expecting a worthwhile morning. What I got was an hour of rambling comments on socialized medicine. As far as living longer was concerned, I would have gotten more benefit by staying in bed that morning!

I'm always intrigued by seminars and recently attended one advertised as "How To Become A Dynamic Salesperson." I went with high expectations. Out of the three hours scheduled for the speaker, about two hours were used trying to convince me that I needed $169 worth of books and cassettes.

Deliver what you promise!

Clearly State Your Purpose: A clear purpose builds rapport. When you get up to speak get your purpose out front in the opening minutes. This is especially important if there has been poor preparation for your speech as far as audience expectation is concerned. When your purpose is dimmest you will be the weakest. Let the audience know in clear simple terms what you have come to say.

This exercise sometimes comes as a minor shock to some speakers—when they find out that they have a rough time finding their purpose. Their material over the years has grown like a collage of bits and pieces of speech fragments; and when they are asked to discuss their material in terms of some framework of purpose, they nearly panic.

Being able to state your purpose clearly will not only give your speech direction, but it will also serve as a way to judge your material. The content that enhances and enlarges your purpose stays. The extra bits of material that hang on like parasites are cleaned out.

A well-defined purpose is a mark of the Charis-magic speech!

In beginning this section I stated that where there is no audience expectation, there will be little audience reaction. In closing I would like to add, where there is audience expectation—when you hear someone say "I've been looking forward to your coming for the past week!"—then you know you have a chance to reach your audience.

Checking Your Bearings: Charis-magic power depends on certain psychological conditions: (1) your ability to "stretch" your expectations and (2) your ability to build a trust relationship with your audience.

This "trust zone" is generated when you give your audience certain assurances to convince them you are the kind of person who *can* be trusted.

1. You are *friendly* and not a threat.
2. You *know* what you are talking about.
3. You are *sincere* and can be believed.
4, You *care* about each one personally.
5. You have a message that will *benefit*.

The key to Charis-magic is synergism, the balanced blending of these assurances to produce an effect that is greater than any individual part.

In the next five chapters, each assurance will be examined and you will be given skills to help you weave them into your speech content and delivery.

Four

How To Develop
A
Charis-Magic Personality

If your audience is going to trust you, they need to be assured that you are friendly. Now, I'm not going to feed you a series of clichés about "smile and the world smiles with you." What is at stake here is something much deeper, because appearing friendly is simply the positive side of the question the audience is really asking—"are you a threat?"

The issue in this chapter and those to follow is how to build trust; and in that area the key to reaching the audience is not so much how friendly you are, but how much of a threat you're not! Being friendly with your audience is really a way of assuring them that you aren't "out to hurt them."

DEALING WITH YOUR PERSONALITY

The Quiet and Reserved Person: If you have basically a quiet and reserved personality on and off the platform, your audience for the most part will feel that they can handle you. Even though you might not come on as "bubbly-friendly," people can feel fairly relaxed around you because your personality is saying, "I'm not a threat to you."

This is one of the reasons why many "quiet" personalities can generate a surprising amount of trust among their audiences. Put to rest once and for all any idea that a Charis-magic speaker can be pigeonholed by some arbitrary set of personality traits.

I have seen powerfully moving speakers who were calm and deliberate in their delivery. On the other hand, I've seen some who were just plain dull. In like manner, I have also heard many "sound and fury signifying nothing" speakers, who spewed a mixture of froth and foam. On the other hand, I've also been moved by some energy-charged speakers who fairly rippled with Charis-magic vibes.

Persuasive power comes by working within the integrity of your personality, not by assuming some model of speaking that is foreign to your true nature. Power can be poured from any vessel, if you know how to tip it.

The Aggressive and Self-Asserting Person: If you have an aggressive and hard-driving personality, you will probably seem threatening to your audience unless you are careful. The reasons for this are fairly obvious. You didn't arrive at your present position by letting people walk all over you. You learned how to use your strength and get results in a world of personal challenges. Sometimes, in order to achieve your ends, you have had to work under the gun, drive your employees to higher production levels, or fight city hall. You had to develop drive and determination.

Now, if you take that raw power and throw it in the face of several hundred strangers in a speaking situation, you will feel immediate resistance. People will feel uneasy around you if you come on with strength that appears threatening; and your audience will have a difficult time trusting you if you make them feel insecure around you.

What is at stake here is not your strength. People admire those who can "make things happen." The issue is how you use your strength! People love to see strength in action; but, and here is the critical point, they don't want to feel that it's being aimed at them.

I am fascinated by Bengal tigers. I have seen them in cages at the circus and have been awed by their beauty and strength. I could watch them by the hour, but if one of them ever got loose and came charging at the stands where I was sitting, I guarantee you my feelings about those cats would undergo a radical change. I'd be running for the nearest exit just as fast as I could move because I don't want that cat all over me with his enormous strength.

When your audience feels threatened, they will draw into their shells and take a defensive position. They will say to you, in effect, "try and get through to me." If your personality drives them into foxholes, your message will have a hard time reaching them.

Many of you who have strong personalities, who work in decision-making, self-starting positions, have learned the secret of handling your strength before an audience. You already know how to break through audience resistance and build trust by assuring the audience you are a friendly and non-threatening speaker; but for others, who are still dealing with the problem, I'd like to offer some suggestions.

BACKING OFF YOUR STRENGTH

In order to make you seem less of a threat, your first step is to back off your strength. I was introduced to this principle while I was earning my college tuition selling cookware. Our sales manager was giving us a demonstration on getting a foot in the door so we could sell our pots and pans.

"Okay, fellows, first put a smile on your face! Let that feeling of confidence start in your toes and go up to your nose! Go to the first house you come to and walk right up and knock on the door ... and then step back a couple of steps."

I had to ask, "Why do we have to step back?"

"Well, let's think about it a minute," he replied patiently,

"Suppose this lady's in the house. She hears a knock on her door. Now what's the first thing that's going to come to her mind?"

"She wants to know who's out there and what he wants," one of the others fired back.

"Right! She doesn't know who you are or why you're there. As far as she knows, you might be there to hurt her. Now what do you think you're going to have to do to get in that house?"

"No big deal," popped up one of the others, "all you have to do is show her you're a nice guy."

"Right, you want her to feel at ease and comfortable around you so you can get your pots and pans in that house, and one of the ways you do that is to back off from that door! Give her some distance so when she opens it you're not right there hovering over her like some hungry vulture. Back off, put some distance between you and her. That's just like shouting out loud to her, "Look, I'm not close enough to hurt you!" She'll feel a lot safer around you and at least you'll have a chance to get in that door and make that sale!"

The aggressive, self-assertive person needs to psychologically back off his strength. This is a known skill to those who have learned to use their power effectively. The shrewd person does not expose all his strength until he needs to call on it. If you run "flat out" all the time, you will have nothing in reserve when you really need it. I have way more horsepower than I need to do the speed limit on the highway, but if I'm passing a car and suddenly find myself in trouble with an oncoming truck barreling down on me, I want to be able to slam that accelerator down to the floor and call on that reserve horsepower to pull me out of danger.

In dealing with your audience you will find that if you come on a little low-keyed, if you have the suggestion of strength but wrap it in a friendly image, you will generate immense drawing power. This is the kind of stuff that Charis-magic power is made of.

Look at my Bengal tiger again. See all that raw, savage power. Stand in awe, but then see how captivated and charmed you become when he rolls over on his back like a playful kitten and yawns. You feel as if you could almost run over to him and pet him. This strong yet enticing strength is what I am suggesting you take to the podium. This wrapping of your personal strength in a friendly image is probably the best understanding of what is meant by a charming personality.

This is a far cry from the "be friendly and smile" approach to reaching your audience. This kind of charming image can't be generated with clichés and nickel and dime suggestions. It must rise out of your control over the energy and drive that pours out of your personality.

WRAPPING YOUR STRENGTH IN A FRIENDLY IMAGE

This technique of wrapping strength in a friendly context, solved a problem in the design of one of my brochures. This will serve as an example of how you might utilize this skill. The lead words on the front of the brochure read, "A New Source of Energy." Inside the brochure, to convey the idea of strength and power, my layout man had pasted a cut-out, full-length photograph that caught me in an explosive moment of my delivery. My coat was flung wide open, my left arm was thrust into the air with my fist clenched and the expression on my face was intense and almost bordered on defiance. It was a picture of pure power, suspended in time by the camera.

As we looked at it, though, we got an uneasy feeling that something was wrong, and then it hit us—the picture was *too* strong. Standing alone and dominating the page as it did it gave the impression of being threatening and overpowering.

We looked for a solution and reluctantly decided to change the photograph. Searching around, we found a simple head shot of me that was smiling and friendly. I looked completely harmless; but when we replaced the power photo with it, the brochure just died; all the life went out of it. Now we had just another, "smile and the world smiles with you" appeal.

Either by chance or instinct, my layout man hit on the solution. He put back the original design and then trimmed the smiling head shot and pasted it right on top of the midsection of the power photo. The effect was instantaneous. You could see power in the background but right up front you were greeted by a smiling face, a friendly wrapping that says, "I may look threatening, but I'm really a nice guy."

SKILLS IN BUILDING A FRIENDLY IMAGE

What follows is in the nature of a checklist to help you determine how well you are doing in building this first assurance with your audience. Whether you consider yourself a quiet or aggressive person, you will find skills to assist you in tuning in to your audience and building trust among them. If you were analyzing a speech, you could look for these features and mark them with an F (friendly) to see how well the speaker is doing in projecting his friendly image.

Dressing For the Occasion: The researchers tell us that people are conditioned to believe certain things about us as a result of the clothes we are wearing. For example, because of the influence of the movies and television, the public tends to believe that a person wearing a dark suit, silk tie and vest is probably a professional; whereas, the man in the plaid jacket and red pants is a used-car salesman.

Granted, this argument is *logically* filled with holes. Certainly, you can't make a man an executive by simply putting a dark blue suit on him. Remember, you are not dealing here with some eternal truth, but with what the public has been conditioned to believe. If your audience reacts to you according to the way they see you, and if they have been led to believe that certain clothes and colors on you indicate some kind of power or lack of it, then you need to take this into consideration in relating to them.

The results of testing show that, in the public's mind, dark colors—dark blue, dark charcoal gray and dark brown—tend to be "power colors." They are associated with people who have authority. Solid black is advised against as almost funereal and threatening.

The blue and grey colors are considered friendly, and the light and white shades are regarded as "lacking any significant authority."

Now this is certainly an oversimplification, but the point is that your clothes are either whispering or shouting something about the kind of person you think you are. As noted, you may want to disregard this and insist that you are your own person and no one can tell you what to wear and what not to wear. That's your right and is certainly an indication of your individuality. But the case being made here is for another way of getting through to your audience, not some attempt to impose on your life style.

For example, you might prefer the dark, conservative power-image; but if you were trying to speak to an audience of Virginia coal miners, you might find it to your advantage to "lighten up" a little. On the other hand, you might be in the middle of a corporate battle where you need to muster every bit of personal and psychological strength you can. That's no time to make an appearance in a sport shirt and brown suede loafers. People tend to react to you according to the way they see you.

A Guideline For Dressing For A Speech: Your choice of dress for a speaking engagement should be in harmony with the purpose of your speech. What have you come to say and do? Do you want to impress the audience primarily with a sense of your authority, warmth or do you just want to be neutral? There should be a harmony between your message and your personal appearance. Your clothes should support and enhance what you have come to accomplish. On the other hand, if your audience has a lot of comments to make about your clothes, they are probably detracting from your message and should be adjusted. You may love to try all the latest styles, but you haven't come to model, you've come to get a message across.

Walk over to your closet at your first opportunity and ask yourself what your clothes are telling others about you. What kind of nonverbal impressions are they signaling to your audience?

Look closely at other speakers. See how their appearance affects your feelings about them before they ever say a word.

Ask if their clothes seem to be in harmony with the meeting and their message, or if their clothes are talking so loudly you can't hear a word they're saying.

One of the most fascinating and creative uses of clothes to establish rapport I've ever seen was in a meeting with Bill Cosby, the gentle comedian. We were doing a homecoming program together at Stetson University in Deland, Florida. The gymnasium was packed with students and alumni. You could smell the excitement and anticipation in the air. Cosby came out to thunderous applause wearing a green warm-up jacket. He sat down on a stool and started his warm routine with the students. About ten minutes into his opening, he complained about being a little warm and unzipped his jacket and peeled it off. Underneath he was wearing a sweat shirt emblazened with the words, *Stetson University*. The students went wild! In that simple act he symbolically said, "Hey, I'm one of you!" His rapport with the students was so strong, he could have read recipes for the next two hours and they would have loved it.

What are you saying with your clothes? Are you enhancing your audience rapport and helping build trust or are you at war with yourself with clothes that fight against you?

Utilizing Your Opening Remarks: How you open your speech can be critical in how well you get through to your audience. You have only one chance to make a first impression. You are introduced and walk up to the podium. The audience for the most part is open, receptive and ready to give you a fair hearing. You start to speak and in the few minutes that follow your audience is going to make some quick decisions:

- whether you are going to be dull or interesting
- whether you are going to have something of value to say or will be just beating the air with a lot of words
- whether they will continue to listen to you or mentally shut you off and think about other things
- whether they like you
- and as if this isn't enough, whether you are the kind of person they can feel at ease and comfortable with, or the kind of speaker "you have to watch out for"

Not that the audience doesn't change its mind during the course of a speech; but it's much easier to get them on your side right from the beginning than have to fight uphill all the way. What are the impressions you will give in your opening moments to assure the audience that you are "friendly" and not a threat?

I have heard some speakers who sound almost arrogant in their opening remarks. I remember one in particular who started by saying, "I know so much about this subject I don't know where to begin." Now, strangely enough, I happen to know he was telling the truth. He had immense knowledge about the topic. In his mind his statement might have been nothing more than an indication of his own confidence and should have been seen as a strength in his speaking ability; but when it flowed to the audience, he came off as a self-centered, conceited bore. He was at war with the audience in the first ten seconds.

One of my earliest speaking engagements was to a convention of public relations directors of a group of American colleges. In preparing my opening remarks I wanted to convey to these professionals that I wasn't going to try to be "slick" in my delivery. I wanted them to know that I respected their ability and knew better than to come on as some "hyped" can of beans. Unfortunately, I expressed this by saying.

"I learned a long time ago not to try to beat a man at his own game. I've learned not to try to kid a kidder, or con a con man or promote a promoter."

It wasn't until years later that I learned that my use of the phrase "to con a con man" put many in the audience on the defensive. They thought I was equating their work with that of a con man and were personally offended. They were not going to listen to a speaker who implied that they were spending their lives deceiving the public. In the first few minutes I was at war with my audience, and I didn't even know it.

Even a humorous opener can set an arrogant tone to your presentation. Here is a classic example:

"You know, when your program chairman was planning this meeting, he wanted someone really special for this spot. He tried to get the most talented man in the state, but unfortunately he was turned down. Then he tried for the best looking man and got turned down again. Finally he went after the most brilliant man . . . and I accepted. I didn't have the heart to turn him down three times in a row."

Watch out for the materials you send winging at your audience in those first few minutes. They can come back to haunt you in your search for Charis-magic power. Let me share some approaches you can use in your openings that will establish you as a friendly and non-threatening speaker.

Learn to Laugh at Yourself: One of the simplest techniques to warm an audience up to you is to poke a little fun at yourself. The simple truth is that people feel more at ease and comfortable with someone who can laugh at himself. When you become the object of your own barbs you show you are not so unapproachable after all. This is especially true if you are a person of strength and authority. Symbolically, when you "pull the beard of the lion" you are saying, "Come on, enjoy him. He won't hurt you."

Share something about yourself that shows you don't take all that talk about how important you are too seriously. Take a swing at your title. I heard a Professor of Education with a doctoral degree open his address to a convention of secretaries by saying, "Some got out of my college *magna cum laude* and some graduated *summa cum laude* but I got out "thank you, Laude!"

Lighten the impact of your title or achievements. Often after my introduction with its panorama of plaudits, I begin by telling this story:

"I guess you noticed in my introduction I was Central Florida's man of the year some years ago. Now that sounds pretty impressive, but I've got to tell you about it. It was quite an evening. The mayor was there and the chief of police and there I was right in the middle getting ready to get my award. During the banquet I couldn't help but overhear a woman sitting next to my wife ask her, How does it feel to be married to the man of the year? I couldn't wait for the answer. After all, I was due a little respect. Would you believe she leaned back to the woman and said,

"Well, honey, that just goes to show you what kind of year it was!"

You might want to take a poke at your speaking ability:

"I hope I do better with this speech tonight than I did last week. It's not that I thought I had done so badly. In fact, a man came up afterwards and gave me a real compliment. He said my speech was like the peace and mercy of God. Now, that's a humbling thing to tell a man. I mean he's talking about my speech being like God! That's no small compliment. I just had to ask him why and he told me.

"He said my speech was like the peace of God because it passeth all understanding, and that it was like his mercy because he thought it was going to endure forever!

Whenever you take the wind out of your own sails, or punch a hole in all the pomp surrounding you, you will find that people will warm up to you. In time you will actually "feel the glow" as it spreads through your audience. This is a glimmer of Charis-magic power. Remember, the greater your place of authority, the stronger your credentials, the more powerful your position, the greater your need to establish that, in spite of it all, you are not a threat. This is simply one technique. You may not feel comfortable with it, but at least experiment with it.

Avoiding the Put-Down. Remember that people don't mind strength if it's not aimed at them. Even so, they don't mind your taking a poke at yourself, but they get uncomfortable when you aim the barbs at them. A put-down is a verbal attack on someone's ego. No matter how graciously the person may seem to be taking it, you can be sure he's feeling a little uneasy. A put-down is a blow to a person's pride and self-esteem, and should be avoided.

I have had my share of them, especially from inept people who are called on to introduce me. "I'd rather hear Dick Milham speak than eat, and I've heard him eat!" and "You probably noticed the size of his nose. Well, he got it fixed, but now his mouth won't work!" and so it goes. I have never felt better for it or closer to a person because of it. You can only complicate your task of presenting yourself as a person who wants to be a friend.

If you really want to bury yourself, take on the whole audience with such classics as, "I know you're out there, I can hear you breathing"; "They told me a lot of you were dumb, but I didn't know you were all deaf!" A couple of shots like this and you can fold it up for the night and head for home.

Lifting Up Your Audience: People feel good about people who give them sincere compliments. We all enjoy compliments. We all need to feel important and be appreciated. The majority of incentive programs are based on some form of recognition whether it be a plaque or a bonus check. What is not as obvious, though, is that an audience can be complimented just like an individual. A speaker who develops this skill has in his hands another tool to build rapport and trust with the audience.

As a speaker, you need to locate some point of group pride, some project, achievement or recent accomplishment they are all delighted with. This may take some digging on your part, but ask questions, observe the surroundings, listen to the conversations. Somewhere you will uncover a bit of Charis-magic dynamite. Sometimes the answer will surprise you.

I was asked to address a plastics firm in Illinois. During their annual banquet I was fishing around for some bit of information that would help me establish a rapport with them. One of the men at the table shared a recent accomplishment that had the plant in high spirits. I knew I had the missing piece and incorporated it into my opening remarks:

"Congratulations to the number one softball team in the city!" They spent the next minute cheering themselves, and I was on my way to a Charis-magic evening.

I know that many of you are aware of the intrinsic danger that goes with this technique. Many have been trained in the old school that advises you to just pay a compliment; that it doesn't matter it is, just find something to say regardless. That reminds me of the new salesman who was trained this way. He knocked at a door and a portly lady answered it. Remembering his boss's advice to pay a compliment, he thought and thought and finally sighed, "You know something, lady? For a fat woman you sweat less than anyone I have ever met!"

When a compliment is reduced to flattery, we don't have

the development of trust, but mistrust instead. A compliment has to be worth its giving. It has to ring with the strength of sincerity and credibility.

How To Give A Sincere Compliment: The secret of giving a sincere compliment to an audience or an individual is simple: Recognize that what the person is trying to tell you is important to him. People are always giving you clues and sending out signals about the things that give them a sense of pride and accomplishment. They wear buttons on their lapels and pins on their blouses. Corporations have trophies on their shelves and plaques on their walls. They are telling you what they want you to recognize and compliment them about.

If you walk into a man's office and he has a shelf lined with tennis trophies, he's not expecting you to gush, "You must be the world's greatest tennis player!" All he needs from you is your observation, "You must really love the game" He'll fill in the rest.

When you are invited to speak at a meeting, *look for the trophy case!* Ask the person inviting you to share some of the plans and accomplishments of the organization. If practical and possible, ask him to mail you their in-house publication or newsletter or any other material related to the business. Search them out. Find some aspect of the group you can compliment in a sincere manner and then work the remarks into your opening comments: "I noticed while reading your newspaper that you are the number one region in sales in your company. That's no small accomplishment and I just want to say, Congratulations!"

Find A Common Experience With Your Audience: You naturally feel closer to a person if you find you have something in common. As a speaker, one of the ways you can build your friendly rapport is to find some experiences that will bind you together with your audience. One way is to mention specific persons, places, events. You will discover that every "specific" will probably ring a bell with someone in the audience. You can start with personal references: "I was born in Brooklyn" *(applause, applause)*, "during the depression of the thirties" *(I've heard my dad talk about that)*, "of immigrant parents" *(So was I!)*, "I graduated from Wheaton College" *(Hey, I used to play basketball against them)*, and married a girl from North Carolina *(Where? Where? I'm from North Carolina!")*.

I opened a management seminar with a large national convenience food store group by sharing: "Being with you store managers brings back a lot of warm memories for me. My dad was a grocer, an immigrant who, with my mother, came to this country looking for the land of opportunity. They opened a little grocery store in Orlando, Florida. As a small boy I used to go with him to the market to pick up fresh vegetables and then to the store to stock the shelves and sweep the floors. I know a little about what it means to pour your life into this business. I am glad I can be a part of it again."

Your life is a gold mine of personal experiences that will help you build friendly rapport with your audiences. Whenever you are faced with a speaking opportunity, search out your memories and you will probably find some experience that will help you pave the way to reaching your audience.

Sometimes, though, you may be hard pressed to come up with some personal experience. In that case, look for an experience involving many people. Golf is an example. I am always going to conventions that have a golf tournament as part of their activities:

"Sorry I arrived too late to get into the golf match. Not that I'm that good at the game. I'm kind of rusty. In fact, I gave it up a couple of years ago after a bad experience. My neighbor, Henry and I used to go out every Saturday afternoon, but he got nearly impossible to play with. In fact I got so fed up one afternoon that I just threw my clubs down and left.

Peggy, my wife asked me what I was doing home so early, so I told her. I asked her if she would play golf with a man who kicked his ball out of the rough, cheated on his score and refused to replace his divots? She said she wouldn't. So I told her, *"neither would Henry!"*

In this chapter I have said that to build a friendly rapport with your audience, you need to relate to them in such a way that they feel comfortable around you. I suggested wrapping your strength in a friendly image, and during these last pages have been giving you some practical guidelines on how to do it.

I have been careful from the very beginning of this chapter to avoid the impression that a friendly person has to come on like some back-slapping, Cheshire-cat grinning, good-old-boy to relate to the audience. This may be totally out of character with your personality. What I have tried to convey is that within the bounds of your integrity as a person, you should make it possible for people to approach you with the feeling that you are not a threat to them.

Key

HELPING A STRONG MAN BECOME STRONGER

I was invited to a regional office of one of our nation's largest insurance companies to have lunch with some of the executives and discuss the details of some speaking assignments I had with them. The atmosphere was cordial. The men were sharing their feelings. The ideas were flowing; and, as they offered me suggestions and guidance, the series of messages were starting to take shape in my mind.

Halfway through the meal, though, we were joined by the regional vice-president and suddenly the mood of the group seemed to change. They became hesistant in speaking out and were more deliberate in their choice of words. The free exchange of ideas was gone and a certain tension filled the air. Every clatter of a dish or movement of any kind seemed to take on exaggerated importance.

I wondered about the radical change and then the obvious hit me; it was his presence, the vice-president's presence that made the sudden difference. He represented authority and power and now that power was thrust into the middle of the group and they weren't able to adequately cope with it or feel comfortable around it. The message that was emanating from that group was "Don't cross the boss in any way; he can hurt you."

Afterwards, I was invited by the vice president to join him in the privacy of his office. During our conversation he mentioned that he was having a problem getting his executives to respond in the staff meetings and mentioned their apparent unwillingness to make any comments on his suggestions. He also was concerned that in his public speaking attempts he always felt that he wasn't getting through to the audience. "It seems to me like they just sit there."

"It's not difficult for me to see why your staff acts the way they do around you," I said, "They're scared stiff of you!" I saw the look of surprise on his face. "I felt it today when you came to lunch. They were chattering away and the moment you arrived they pulled into their protective shells. Right or wrong, in their eyes, you appear as some kind of threat.

"That's news to me," he replied. "As long as I've known some of these men, I've never felt they were afraid of me. Sure I make demands and expect results, but I'm not in the habit of threatening anyone."

"Not from your perspective, but let's look at it from theirs." I took out my pen, took one of his yellow pads and wrote down the five assurances—*friendly*, *knowledgeable*, *sincere*, *caring*, *benefits*. "These are the ingredients needed to build a relationship of trust. Now let's look at them and see how your staff might score you.

"Let's get the obvious ones out of the way. I have no doubt you are a man who knows his job and means what he says, so I'm checking off *knowledgeable* and *sincere*. That brings me to *benefits* and at this point I'm inclined to believe your staff see you as a whole stack of benefits. You're the key to job promotions, salary increases and probably the executive wash room.

"The problem here, though, is that you are also the possible source of the loss of these benefits; you can fire them, and that makes you seem a threat, a tiger on the loose.

"Whether you intended it or not, they feel your power aimed at them and they are uncomfortable."

"I don't know why they should feel that way," he interjected, "I certainly don't go around threatening them."

"Not verbally, but it's implied by the lack of other assurances. Look at *caring* and *friendly*. What in your relationship with your staff tells them that you are concerned with them as individuals and that your strength is not meant to be a threat?"

"I might also say, without ever having heard you, that this is also the key to your speaking problem. You are unconsciously probably coming on to your audience in such a way that your power is being aimed right down their throats. If that's the case you can count on the fact that they have retreated to their foxholes, and they're not coming out until the shooting is over."

I spent time with him sharing the skills of this chapter and Chapter Seven on caring. I did all I could in a short time to help him draw back his strength and wrap it in a friendly image. I talked to him about having a few laughs at his own expense at the next board meeting and showed him how to tone down his strength in his speech openers. I suggested lightening his dress and sharing personal experiences in his content.

I saw him several months after that at one of the meetings and he told me what a tremendous difference those simple skills had made in his ability to relate to his staff and his audiences.

"Strange, when I think back," he said, "how I thought I was a friendly person and all the time I appeared like a man-eating tiger!"

A WORD OF SUMMARY

The experience of Charis-magic power depends on the speaker's ability to build a relationship of trust with his audience. This trust zone is woven together with five assurances that are intended to convince the audience that the speaker is the kind of person who can be trusted.

The first assurance is that the speaker is friendly. In this chapter I suggested that you can build a friendly rapport by wrapping your strength in a friendly image and shared some skills on how to do it.

In the next chapter we will look at the second of these assurances, the speaker is knowledgeable, he knows what he is talking about.

EPILOGUE

In the folklore of antiquity there is a story about the Sun and the North Wind debating as to which one had the greater strength. They decided to settle the argument with a contest.

Below them they saw a man wearing a jacket, walking along a quiet country road.

"The one of us who can take that jacket off him will be the stronger," they agreed.

The North Wind went first with his frigid tentacles. He lashed his icy fury down on the man trying to rip the jacket off his body; but the harder he blew and the more furiously he pounded against the man, the tighter the man drew his jacket around him to protect himself.

Finally, the North Wind in a rage gave up and turned to the Sun, "He will never give up his jacket. There will be no winner."

The Sun made no reply but simply directed his warmth at the freezing man. Slowly he increased his heat on him, gently bathing him in surges of thawing warmth. The man started to loosen his grip on his jacket, then he unbuttoned it and finally, under the full strength of the Sun's energy, flung it off and exposed himself to its full intensity.

Two men were having a debate about the best way to use their strength . . .

 **Five**

The Charis-Magic Power of Showing You're a Pro in the Know

Years ago, while heading for a speech debate in college, our bus passed a magnificent, sprawling tree. I didn't have the slightest idea what kind it was so I turned to our speech instructor and asked him.

"Oh, it's very rare in this part of the country," he said. "It's a camphor tree. Have you ever seen or heard of one before?"

"No, sir, that's my first one."

He went on to give me a long, detailed and fascinating history of the tree, how it came to this country, its unique characteristics, its commercial uses, and so on. Needless to say, I was tremendously impressed and just had to interrupt to ask:

"Where did you learn so much about camphor trees? You must have been raised with a yard full!"

"A yard full!" he laughed, "Milham I've never seen a camphor tree!"

"What do you mean?" I exploded, "For the last hour you've been telling me all about . . ."

"Hold it, Milham. I'm going to give you your lesson for today. If the people around you don't know any more about a subject than you do, you can become an immediate expert. Who's going to challenge you?"

Remember that the next time you hear someone speaking on a subject that is foreign to you. You had better determine whether he knows what he is talking about, or whether he is giving you the old "camphor tree snow job!"

Your audience has a right to ask what gives you the right to be up there speaking on the subject. How do they know you're not just filling the room with hot air? If the subject is one the audience has very little knowledge of, they are even more inclined to ask you to drag out your credentials and prove that you know what you are talking about. No one wants to be operated on by a Doctor who keeps dropping his scalpel.

That's why another necessary assurance you must give your audience to build trust is "I know what I am talking about." Ways to get that message across to your audience will be explored in this chapter. You will see the critical importance of your Introduction, be shown skills of building authority all through your speech, and learn the secret of how to give a technical speech to a non-technical audience.

ESTABLISHING YOUR RIGHT TO SPEAK IN YOUR INTRODUCTION

The building of your right to speak is not only meant to assure your audience that you are not "taking them for a ride," but is also intended to draw them to you in a trust relationship. There really is power in knowledge. Just like the person with a strong personality, you have a certain fascination to others if you are an expert or authority on a subject. If your knowledge is going to help build your credibility, though, it must also be packaged in a friendly image.

Pure knowledge is hard to swallow if the speaker uses it like a club to show his superior mentality or make his point. Just like the assertive personality it must be wrapped in a friendly image or it will drive the listener away. Certainly there appears to be a problem with how to establish your credentials without "blowing your own horn;" but that's the beauty of a well-prepared Introduction. It will establish your right to speak, give reasons why you should be trusted and believed, show you as a "pro in the know," and it is not from your own lips.

This most critical facet of building trust in you and your right to speak as an authority on the subject is seldom recognized for what it is. The Introduction is not something that is arbitrarily tagged on to the beginning of your speech; it is an indispensable part of the total impact of your message. You must get in control of it!

Nothing will kill you quicker as a speaker than to have someone say, "Our speaker needs no introduction." That might be the case in some rare instances, but in most cases you need all the introduction you can get. As you might remember from an earlier chapter, "where there is no audience expectation you will get very little audience reaction." *Key*

Your Introduction establishes you as a person qualified to address the audience. Without this assurance you will lack credibility, and without credibility, your foundation for building trust is undermined.

Preparing Your Own Introduction: For years I suffered through the agony of wondering what was going to be said about me before I got up to speak. Now I realize that I should never have wasted my energy that way. I should have been spending that time concentrating on the message. It wasn't long until I learned a cardinal rule of audience preparation from an "old pro" in the business—*prepare your own Introduction!*

Who knows better than you what information will be vital in establishing your credentials? You should not leave the writing of your Introduction to chance or to someone scratching out some facts about you on a napkin five minutes before he gets up to introduce you.

Prepare your own Introduction! Mail it in advance. Almost insist that it be used, and when you go to the meeting, carry an extra copy with you. You can be certain that sometime, somewhere, on some occasion you will hear somebody say, "I misplaced it," or "I never received it" or "I have it, but it's in my other briefcase."

Later in this chapter I will share a sample Introduction with you as an aid and guide to help you prepare your own Introduction.

Preparing the Person Introducing You: If at all possible, meet the person who is going to introduce you before the event. Let him know how delighted you are that he will be setting the stage and preparing the audience for your speech. Impress on him how important he is to your success and let him know how much you are counting on him to help you.

Go over the Introduction with him and make sure that he includes those items that are of importance in establishing your right to speak to that particular group on that particular subject. Some people might get a little hard-nosed about what they had prepared already; but stick by your guns. You wouldn't consider letting him get up and give the first five minutes of your speech so don't give in and let him do what he wants to do with this critical aspect of your total message.

Most people who are called on to introduce speakers are usually a little shaky about the task. They were given a part on the program, or ended up with the job by virtue of their office, or because so-and-so couldn't make it. Granted, there are some well-qualified persons who do an admirable job in making an Introduction, but it is better to assume that the Introducer would appreciate some help. You will know immediately in talking with him how much direction he will require.

How To Make An Introduction: In the event that you find yourself as an Introducer, let me set out a few practical guidelines to help you check out your technique.

First, remember that your prime responsibility is to introduce the speaker. Keep the Introduction short and resist the temptation to make a speech yourself or become a comedian. I cannot register the hours of pain I have experienced listening to some poor comedian go through a stack of stale jokes. Humor is fine if it enhances the introduction of the speaker, but it should never appear as a warm-up act.

Second: Remember that the purpose of the Introduction is to show that the speaker is qualified to speak on the subject. If you have been provided with a biographical sketch,then it is your responsibility to read through it and select those items that will help establish the speaker's authority on his subject. If you have waited until the last minute and find that you don't have a biographical sketch, then it's back to the paper napkins.

Third: Save the name of the speaker for the very last words in your Introduction, ". . . and now our guest for the evening, Dick Milham!" and then start the applause. This will signal the speaker that it's time for him to come to the platform. Make a quiet exit, but stay within sight of the speaker. Many times, speakers like to make some response to your Introduction and will be looking for you. This means, don't introduce and run. There is nothing quite as embarrassing to a speaker as discovering his audience has started to walk out on him.

How To Overcome A Poor Introduction: No matter how hard you try to control your Introduction, you have no assurance of what the final outcome will be. So, you had better be ready to pick up the pieces. About the time you think you've heard them all, a new one comes along.

Convention of 3000 Young People: ". . . I was handed this piece of paper on my way up here so I could introduce the speaker . . . but the light is so bad I can't read it . . . well, who cares? . . . the name doesn't matter. Come on up here . . . whatever your name is . . . and speak to us!"

A State Convention: " . . . when I heard how much we were paying this speaker, I couldn't believe it! No one's worth that much! Hell, I'd do it for half that much and still feel I was taking you for a ride!"

A National Convention: " . . . now I've never heard this speaker. They tell me he is good, but who knows? I just wanted you to know that I didn't have anything to do with inviting him, so if he bombs out . . . don't blame me."

At times like these you have no alternative but to introduce yourself; to "blow your own horn." It's better to take a chance with the audience thinking you're a little sold on yourself, then leave them wandering around in a fog as far as your right to speak is concerned.

First: Resist the temptation to "get back" at the Introducer. This is tough; especially if you have a strong ego and feel you have been attacked on some personal level. I remember one occasion when I ignored a particularly crude Introduction. A man came up to me afterwards and commented, "I really respect the way you handled that situation. I'll always remember you for what you didn't say. Personally, I would have busted him in the mouth!"

If the truth were known, I would have enjoyed responding to him the way a Pastor friend did after he was subjected to particularly rude treatment. He went to the podium and opened by saying:

"Now I know what the Philistines felt like when they were slain by the jaw of a jackass."

Second: Introduce yourself. Establish your right to be heard and build some authority into your presence. "You are probably wondering why I have been invited here to speak tonight, and you have every right to ask. Let me introduce myself and my subject and share a few credentials with you." The audience will respect your right at this point, especially in the light of your Introduction.

Structuring A Basic Introduction: You may have already developed a working Introduction, but for those who haven't here is a basic structure and some guidelines:

1. List all the items that come to mind under each of the following headings. Don't worry about being selective. This is just a preliminary move. Later you will only include those items that are the most relevant in supporting your right to speak.

  A. *Your Present Position:* Name of the company and position or positions you have with them.

  B. *Former Positions:* Put them all down now and later you can screen them for their value in your Introduction.

  C. *Education, Professional Affiliations, Writings:* This is the "power portion" of your Introduction. It is here that you will establish most clearly your right to speak.

D. *Special Recognitions:* List all the awards, commendations, honors, etc that have come your way.

E. *Personal Notes:* Family, Civic Clubs, hobbies, etc. These items are primarily used when you are speaking in a situation and on a subject that is personal and not related to your professional and business expertise. These items also can be used to warm up an audience under certain conditions.

F. *Name of Your Subject:* What is the purpose of your speech?

G. *Your Name:* Will appear only one time at the very end of your Introduction and serve as your signal to get up and speak.

2. You are now ready to structure your outline. Keep in mind that you are not putting together a biographical sketch, but a short, concise piece that will have authoritative impact on your audience. Begin by settling item F, *Name of Your Subject.* This might sound strange at first, but until you decide what you are speaking on, you will not have a way of determining which items are relevant to support your knowledge of the subject.

The guiding rule that you will use in distilling the material is, "Does this item add to my authority to speak on this subject?" Now apply the rule. Start weeding out the non-essentials and material that have little authoritative value. Come up with a draft of about 200-250 words (a single page double-spaced). Continue to change and improve it in terms of the subject you are going to speak on. Then use it, Test it at your next meeting. See how you feel about it and how it seemed to prepare the audience for you and your subject.

3. Even though the main intent of the Introduction is to establish your authority to speak on the subject, it can also serve some other ends. For instance it can be used to help build rapport with the audience by adding small phrases that will strengthen your relationship to them.

For instance, if I am speaking to a Real Estate group I add the phrase "a Real Estate broker himself" since I do have these credentials in Florida. If I'm speaking to an education group, I mention, "he received his MA from Stetson University, where he served as an instructor in the extension program for six years."

In this sense, the Introduction should be flexible and throb with vitality. It should be treated as a living force that prepares the way for a speaking force. Treat it with respect. It is not superficial to your presentation, but an integral part of it. Of all kinds of advice I could give to help you as a speaker, this one would be high on the list: "Get control of your Introduction!"

BUILDING AUTHORITY THROUGHOUT YOUR SPEECH

Besides the Introduction, there are other techniques of helping you establish your right to speak on a subject. These involve the content of your material and how you can introduce elements into that content to give the audience the assurance that you know what you are talking about.

Injecting Your Credentials Naturally: You should deliberately drop references to your authority and experience throughout your speech. This is not a matter of bragging, but of continually assuring the audience that you are an authority. The secret of handling this successfully is in how you weave the references into the speech. They should be almost casual and introductory in nature to something else you want to say.

In my opening remarks to the state convention of the Florida Association of Community Colleges, I mentioned that, "while I was working on my Ph.D. at the University of North Carolina, one of my professors gave me an assignment . . . an assignment that turned out to be one of the most mind-challenging experiences I have ever been up against . . . " I went on to tell the story that set the theme for the meeting. As important as the story, though, was the injection of the assurance of authority in the opening phrase. I was saying to all those educators, "I have a right to be here. I've paid my dues and deserve to be heard."

Weave the power of authority throughout your speech. Drop it like explosive bursts of energy into the content of your remarks. Feel the audience respond as they explode. What you have here is a small sample of Charis-magic power.

Make a list of power phrases that you can use in future speeches. Go over your experiences, education, recognitions and the like, and create introductory phrases with them. Don't be concerned now about what they will introduce. That will come later.

Now get your power out in front of you. Come up with ten phrases or passing comments and weave two of them into the content of your next speech. You will soon find that they will flow naturally into the content of your delivery and will begin creating power for you.

Mentioning Authoritative Persons: You probably have accused someone along the way of being a name dropper—a person who tries to impress you by mentioning important and powerful people in their conversations. The principle's not bad, just the way some handle it. Name dropping is a powerul technique of establishing your authority and expertise.

First, weave into your speech any personal experiences you may have had with power persons. You may have noticed how I introduced one of my illustrations in the last chapter by saying:

"One of the most fascinating and creative uses of clothes to establish rapport I've seen was in a meeting with Bill Cosby, ... *we were doing a homecoming program together* . . ." Although I didn't come right out and say it openly, my reference to being on the same program with Cosby was a power indicator that said I wasn't your garden variety speaker.

Second, You are fully aware of the power of endorsements in the business world and in advertising. Well, quoting an authority is a technique of producing power that borders on an endorsement. Symbolically, all the authority and prestige of the person being quoted is transferred to you. You are in essence saying that since this authority agrees with you, that gives you the right to make the statement. A word of caution: be sure the person you choose to quote is a real authority on the subject and not just a popular figure. Quoting Merv Griffin on the state of the American economy will not be too convincing and will not produce the desired power.

Examine the content of your material. See if you can

strengthen its feeling of authority by quoting a recognized figure. Be careful of controversial figures, though, because they can hurt you in the minds of those in the audience who don't agree with them. If they don't like the person you quoted, they may end up not liking you, especially if they feel you two are "birds of a feather."

Avoid the temptation of making a textbook out of your speech by supporting your every comment with a quote. A few well-chosen references to power figures are probably more than enough in a basic speech presentation. After all, the audience has come to hear what you have to say, not get a consensus of where the authorities stand.

Use The Results of Statistics, Surveys and other Sources: People are intrigued with numbers and charts. There is something almost artistic about a diagram with colored lines and intricate patterns, and surveys generate the power to arouse and satisfy curiosity.

All of these techniques can be used to produce authoritative power. Use them! and introduce them from sources that are also authoritative:

"In a recent survey in the *Harvard Business Review* . . ."
"According to the latest Harris poll . . ."
"In an article in this issue of *Time* magazine . . ."

My own publicity includes the phrase, "In a recent article on the front page of *The Wall Street Journal* . . ."

A word of caution: don't fall in love with statistics. Nothing can kill the vitality of your presentation faster than trying to explain a chart or survey point for point. Unless this is the prime purpose of your speaking, avoid going into detail. Just draw the conclusions that you need to support your position and summarize them. Keep the vitality of your presence before the audience and be careful not to allow yourself to be submerged in a sea of numbers. At the end of this section I will deal with the problem of how to deliver a technical speech to a non-technical audience.

Doing Your Own Survey: By quoting the results of your own survey, you can add authority as well as credibility to your speech. Your involvement in getting the results will also show your audience how you have tried to prepare for them in a personal way. Here are some possible examples of how you can weave this power into your speech:

"I was wondering how the increase in water bills was affecting the restaurant business, so I called several of the owners here in town and here's what they told me . . ."

"I was asked to talk about *Youth Facing the 21st Century.* Now I feel I know something about technology because of my position as an engineer with my company, but I wasn't sure I could speak for our young people, so I took the afternoon off one day and spent it at the High School asking questions. What I learned opened my eyes and I think will be of interest to you . . ."

One of the most energy-filled surveys can be the one you carry out right there on the spot as you are speaking. One of my contracts for several years has been with a large company that sells clothes through home parties. Last summer, in every one of their seven zones, I opened my seminars with them by asking, "Why did you join the company?" The response was always varied, alive, spontaneous and the participation helped me develop an immediate rapport with them. There was then a willingness on their part to let me be heard.

More important, though, the results of the survey gave me a springboard to use for a detailed presentation of how to recruit women according to their needs.

If you try this technique, be sure to come up with a question that is relatively easy to answer or you can be standing there with the proverbial egg on your face. It is not beneath a good speaker to have several people prepared beforehand to participate. Sometimes this is called priming the pump, or breaking the ice, or covering your bets. Whatever, it is certainly better than standing up there with perspiration pouring down your face.

Show A Knowledge of Other Viewpoints: You generate authority when you demonstrate that you are aware of other viewpoints on the subject. One of the major resistances going on in some members of the audience is the unspoken thought, "Yea, I hear him, but he probably doesn't understand the other side of that argument." You can "pull the teeth" of that resistance by showing that you are familiar with all sides of an issue: "I am fully aware that my views are not held by everyone. I have tried to consider all the evidence, and even though I have studied all the alternatives and the arguments that support them, I still contend that . . ."

Sometimes the issue is such that you have to go into the lion's den to assure yourself of appearing as a knowledgeable authority:

"I have tried to be fair in my evaluation of his stand on this issue. In fact, I called him to make sure I understood his position. I thanked him for spending time with me and sharing his views and for making sure I understood him correctly. On the basis of that conversation, I want to make the following comments . . ."

Researching Your Audience: No matter how much of an authority you might be on a subject, an audience will cut you off if you haven't done your homework. You can lose a lot of personal power simply by not being informed about the people you are talking to, the product or service they are involved in, and the purpose of their meeting.

Know your audience! Ask in advance for newsletters, magazines, annual reports, advertising materials, etc. Get your hands on any kind of information that will help you "tune in" to the people you are trying to reach with your message. Sometimes a simple act or statement will overshadow every bit of so-called authority that you bring with you and unknowingly shut the door of power in your face.

I saw a hotel lose a lot of potential business because they served rice at a banquet of a potato association. I saw a professional speaker lose his credibility as a man with good sense when he kept telling his audience how great it was to be with the finest insurance executives in the country. They were C.P.A.s.

On the other hand, you can gain much power by demonstrating to your audience that you have "checked them out" as any smart speaker would do. They cannot help but gain an appreciation for your expertise as you make personal references to the company, its products and personnel: "In studying your annual report I was impressed to discover that you are the fastest growing tool manufacturer in the country!"

"In last month's issue of your company's paper, I read an article by your president where he has asked for a full commitment to excellence in your work and products. What a tremendous and challenging goal!"

Every reference of this kind, where you demonstrate your personal research of your audience, adds to your authority in your subject. They figure that if you have taken that much time to be accurate about them, you certainly have checked out your own material.

Find the references. Incorporate them into your remarks *Key* and feel their Charis-magic effect.

HOW TO GIVE A TECHNICAL SPEECH TO A NON-TECHNICAL AUDIENCE

I recently came across an article written to engineers warning them to be wary of the advice of so-called speech experts when it comes to giving a technical speech to other engineers. The author suggested that the typical advice is good for the college freshman giving a little talk, but not for engineers trying to get across technical knowledge.

He argues that the technical speech is not meant to be entertaining or friendly. It is, by its very nature, aggressive because it seeks to show the speaker's technical superiority over the others who are listening.

His advice, in summary, was to forget the audience. "You're not there to entertain them but to display your superior knowledge. For that reason you should concentrate on giving facts, data, and any detail that will enhance your position. Don't even worry about any gestures. The audience should be taking notes, not looking at you."

If an analysis were made of this model speech with our assurances, you would come up with almost all K's (knowledge), possibly a few B's (benefits), but no F's (friendly), S's (sincere) or C's (caring). As far as the speaker himself is concerned, his role is simply to relate the knowledge in the pages. He has the same value as a printed report.

Now, maybe this is really the case when technician meets technician, although I don't feel that it has to be. What concerns me is the end result of this conditioning when a technical speaker is suddenly faced with a non-technical audience. How do you handle technical knowledge when to the layman's mind the data is incomprehensible, the language is untranslatable and the concepts are indescribable?

Obviously, everything I am advocating in this book is applicable to producing a strong speech. What I want to do here is simply zero in on a few suggestions that will improve the impact of a speech that has the handicap of a lot of technical data as an intricate part of its composition.

1. *Get an interesting title:* The layman's mind is not going to become too excited about "The Functional Value of the Laser Beam" but you might have a chance with "The Laser Beam—Stairway to the Stars."

2. *Use handouts:* If you have to utilize some technical statistics or data then have them printed and handed out and then summarize what they mean in simple terms. Do not succumb to the temptation of getting into the detail. The natural inclination of the technical mind is to document everything with proof positive. You are going to have to learn that the audience will take your word for it. They don't have much option. They certainly are not equipped to deal with the technical explanation. Once you have established your authority as an expert, then simply bring them your conclusions.

3. *Use a prop if it will simplify:* Props are excellent in helping people see what you are talking about. I still remember a speech on the coaxial cable because the speaker brought a section of it with him. Instead of a lot of technical talk about its structure and the effect of weather on it, he translated it into simple terms that were interesting: "Did you know that a fully equipped tube of cables is about three inches wide and can carry 32,400 two-way conversations simultaneously?" This is an example of technical results being explained in non-technical terms.

4. *Use a strong opener:* Find a way to translate the technical talk into an illustration that has shock value. For instance, take our Laser beam talk. Suppose the speaker, when he gets to the podium, asks for someone to lend him a diamond ring. He holds it up and says, "This is the hardest substance known to

man, but do you know that we have the ability to take a little beam of light and burn a hole right through it!''

5. *The Power Principle:* After years of trying to help people get their technical messages across, there is one principle that has emerged as the most potent one available: *Don't tell people what it is, tell them what it does!* You might ask two men to tell what a television set is. The first might explain in great scientific detail its complex makeup and structure. The other man might just walk over to it and turn on the knob and say, "A television brings pictures into my house." Both men would be right. One told you what it is scientifically, the other man told you what it *does practically.*

During one of my appearances for a manufacturer of men's hair products, I was approached by a chemist with the company who was scheduled to appear on the program. He explained that he was assigned the task of explaining to the hair sytlists and barbers a new line of products and what made them work.

His concern was that his speech was loaded with so much technical language and chemical formulas and the like, that he would come off boring or at best leave them in the dark about the products.

We sat together over a cup of coffee and I asked him to give me his speech and explain the products to me: "Let me hear what you will be telling them. As you know, I'm more of a layman then any of them, and if you can get through to me, they'll be easy for you."

He started his speech and a few minutes into it came up with a long chemical term. "Hold it, I don't understand what that means." He started to give me a technical explanation of the technical term and again I cut in, "No, that's worse." He tried again, and the more he explained the more frustrated he became until he finally erupted in exasperation, "There's no way I'm ever going to make you understand!"

"Well, maybe there is. Tell me. What does this chemical do?" He started another technical explanation and I stopped him. "No, I don't mean that, I mean what will it do to my hair if I use it? When I touch my hair what will I notice if anything as a result of using that chemical?"

"Well, your hair will be softer."

"Softer, now that's a term I can really understand. What else?"

"Well, it will be easier to comb." I could see his mind begin to fit the pieces together. "...and it will reduce the tangles."

"Now you're getting it... don't tell me what this product is chemically, just tell me what it will do for me practically! If you have to, you can mention all the chemicals you want, but don't you leave without telling me what difference they will make in my hair."

He applied the principle and that night came across with a live and vital presentation of what the products would do for the customers. He told them a little about what they are, but a whole lot about what they do.

When you get ready to deliver a technical speech, think of the B's (benefits) and you will be on your way to relating your speech to where the people live.

Thinking Back Over the Chapter: The next time you have an opportunity to listen to a speaker, ask yourself in what ways he has established his right to speak on the subject. Analyze the effect of his Introduction. Did it prepare you to accept the man as an authority on the subject? What did the speaker say in his remarks that reinforced his right to be heard? How did he use quotes, statistics, surveys and the like?

Next, turn your attention to your own material. Using the techniques we used earlier, transcribe a speech and go through it marking it with K's (knowledge) to locate the authority elements in it. Do they come through naturally and do they have any impact in building your relationship with the audience as a man who knows what he is talking about?

Charis-magic power is the total culmination of a lot of forces. The major ones we have called assurances. When these assurances are woven together to build a relationship of trust with the audience, Charis-magic power is not far behind. You have been introduced to two of these assurances—*friendly* and *knowledgeable*. In the next chapter you will meet the third, *sincere*.

 **Six**

The Charis-Magic Impact
of
Speaking Sincerely

When I was growing up, there was a popular song sung by every young lover, "Are You Sincere?" The song was a lament, a plea, an asking for assurance that the lover's lover really meant what he was saying. It was not enough to just hear the words.

Words to an audience must come wrapped in an assurance that you really mean what you are saying. Charis-magic power is dependent on your ability to show that you are sincere. If the audience feels ripples of deception in your presentation, or senses that somehow it is not getting the whole story, or gets the impression that your words and actions don't ring true, it will shut you out.

97

Notice, I didn't say if you really *are* deceptive, I said if the audience *feels* you are. Of course, their feeling that you might not be sincere certainly doesn't make it so; but if you are giving that impression, you must find out why and deal with it. Charis-magic results can only flourish in this assurance that you mean what you say.

FINDING A MEANING FOR THE WORD

A word like "sincere" takes you into a mire of related terminology that would warm the heart of a romanticist but drive someone who thinks in concrete terms almost out of his mind. Suddenly you are surrounded by such words and phrases as, "credible," "trustworthy," "believable," "reliable," "dependable," "worthy of belief," "entitled to confidence" and on and on.

Because of this profusion of words, this whole chapter could be lost in a sea of terminology that keeps doubling back on itself. To deal with this assurance of sincerity, and to give you a hook to hang this chapter on, I want to deal simply and primarily with the word itself and its meaning and impact in building Charis-magic power.

I'm not one for getting bogged down in delving into the meanings of words, but there is something especially revealing about the origin of the word "sincere" that will give you an important clue to the intent of this chapter.

The word originally came to us from the Greek language. In ancient Greek cultures, one of the most respected artists was the sculptor. Many of the ancient greats achieved lasting reputations for the beauty and craftsmanship of their work. The true and talented artist was highly respected and sought after. As in every business, though, there were those who sought to cut corners to increase business.

Traditionally, if a sculptor chipped a piece of marble he was working on in such a way that it cut into the work and would show up as a flaw in the finished product, he would destroy the work and start again. There were others, though, who would simply try to cover up the flaw and pass the work off as a perfect product. To do this, they would take wax and melt it into the chipped place in the marble. When the spot was polished the flaw was invisible to the naked eye and looked just like the marble.

In time, the Greeks started to make note of this deceptive practice and started to identify the real craftsman and artist as the man who created his works sin (without) cere (wax), the words that we eventually got our one word from—sincere. The sincere artist was the man who created his works without wax. When you looked at his product you could be assured that what you saw was what you got. There were no hidden attempts to deceive and trick.

The sincere person is one who is what he appears to be. You know where he stands and how he feels. Relax, there aren't any hidden clauses, booby traps or hooks in his personality. He is out front and what you see is what you get. Interestingly enough, our contemporary dictionaries include in their definitions of the word the phrases, "being in reality what he appears to be," and "just a revealing of what one feels, thinks and sees and no more."

The sincere speaker appears to his audience in such a way that he assures them that he is who he is and he means what he says. You might not believe what he has to say, but you know and sense that he believes, and herein is a critical distinction that must be made. What is at stake in this matter of sincerity is not the content of the message, but the intent of the speaker. At this point it is not a question of whether your message is true or not but whether you come across as believing it is true.

The public in general has already learned to make this distinction. They speak about a person being sincerely wrong, meaning that in their minds what he believes is wrong, but that he really believes it! This is a situation where you have sold yourself, but nobody has bought the product.

At a conference in Atlanta, one of the speakers, a young executive new to public appearances, asked me, "Does sincerity count?"

"Certainly it does," I answered, "It counts a lot, but it is not enough! If you want to reach your audience you must have some knowledge and authority in your content."

Sincerity is only one of the assurances needed to build

Charis-magic power. It is an indispensable one, but to it must be added all the others, especially knowledge. You not only want your audience to say that you mean what you say, you also want them to say that you know what you are talking about. Don't ever buy the cliché that all you need to do in order to be a good speaker is to be sincere. That might get you through your speech, but it won't take the customers home with you.

MEETING A SPECIAL DIFFICULTY

I have a certain feeling of personal frustration in talking about techniques to make you seem sincere. If the problem was one of not enough knowledge, I could point you to the books and the experts to correct the deficit; but when it comes to being sincere, the very suggestion that it can be acted out is in contradiction to its definition—being in reality what one appears to be.

In Charis-magic speaking, the man cannot be separated from his message. He is committed to believe what he is saying. In this sense, sincerity is the impression, the "vibe," the assurance that the speaker buys his own message. He puts the weight of all he is as a person behind it.

For this reason, the impact of sincerity usually comes through the speaker's revelation of his own personal experiences; and this is dependent upon the speaker being able and willing to expose and show pieces of himself to his audience. In all honesty, I have found that many speakers find it very uncomfortable to talk about themselves in a personal way. In their minds, it is hard enough to stand before the audience alone and vulnerable without "looking for trouble" by exposing their personal insights.

But power comes from trust, and trust comes out of a relationship between the audience and the speaker. This trust relationship is built on the kind of "stuff" that feelings are made of. You can communicate more with a touch, whether it is physical or emotional, than with an academic discourse that fails to reveal anything about the speaker and does nothing to reach the listener.

The techniques I will be sharing with you in this chapter are different than those you received in discussing friendly and knowledgeable. What I am suggesting now is that you put yourself on the line. "What you see is what you get" requires showing; and what has to be shown is not just your mind, but your feelings, emotions, opinions—the kind of "stuff" that builds trust.

Sincerity requires you to share concerns that you are committed to as important in your life; committed to, not just involved with. You are being called on to expose those areas of your personal life that really make a difference; not simply to talk about your hobbies or what you do in your spare time.

These personal experiences will be the prime source of the material you will need to build the assurance of sincerity with your audience. In this chapter you will be given some skills on how to relate yourself to your audience as a sincere person; and how to take your sincerity into the most difficult speaking arena of them all, the hostile audience.

SKILLS IN SHOWING YOUR SINCERITY TO YOUR AUDIENCE

Expressing Views As Your Own: An audience feels closer to a speaker who shares something personal with them. There is an ancient proverb that says, "to make a friend, tell him a secret about yourself." This symbolic welcoming of an audience into your private life has power in generating a strong rapport with them. Now I'm not advocating that you make the podium some kind of a confessional booth, but I am suggesting that it can be powerfully used as a warm fireside room where you can make a friend.

An audience always feels a little detached from a speaker who is always documenting everything he says by quoting someone else. "According to . . .", In the view of . . .," "In his latest book on . . ." Sometimes, in listening to one of these speakers I just want to cry out, "What about you? What do you believe? Share your feelings and your views!"

If, as a speaker, you are always giving the impression that you cannot make a statement without putting it into someone else's mouth, the audience will begin to wonder if you've got anything to share personally or whether you are just pulling from a filing cabinet located in your head. Sincerity requires personal sharing.

Key

Several years ago I was doing some seminars for a highly technical industry. They had realized the need to develop some increased awareness in their staff and employees in the areas of self-esteem, relating to others, and dealing with stress. The staff member put in charge of picking me up at the airport and escorting me throughout the day seemed nice enough. He was a career engineer with about fifteen years of experience under his belt, but he had recently been moved up into an administrative post with the company.

Early into our conversation I found that I was having an extremely difficult time getting a straight answer out of him. Everything he said was attached to some kind of qualification or reservation. "Well, that's hard to say without having all the facts right here with me . . ." or "We haven't been able to determine that yet with any degree of accuracy that would let us say for certain . . ." I felt as if I was talking to a machine that kept saying, "I'm sorry but that does not compute!"

That afternoon I was introduced to the first group of about two hundred engineers. I felt good about the presentation and yet I wanted to adjust my material for the next group in the event that I could make it stronger. I asked my host, "Well, what did you think about the session? How did you think it went?"

A curious expression came across his face. "I'm not really sure," he responded slowly, "Possibly it was good and possibly it needs improving."

"I'm aware of all the possibilities, but what did you think about it personally?"

"Well, I'm really not sure how to answer that."

"But you must have some opinion," I pressed.

"Would you wait one minute, please," he finally responded, "I will be back shortly." He disappeared, but in a few moments returned beaming all over.

"You did excellently" he reported, "the response of our employees was excellent!"

I looked down and in his hands he had a stack of computer cards. I asked him about them and if they had anything to do with his evaluation of my session.

"Well, each person was required to fill one out after the session and evaluate the speaker according to his speech and its content. I just finished running them through the machine and tabulating them."

He looked up at me as close to being enthusiastic as he could get. "We are pleased with the results. Your speech was excellent."

Late in the day, as we were headed back to the airport, we had an opportunity to get to know each other better and to share some of our feelings about things that matter. It was toward the end of that conversation that I asked:

"Do you remember when I asked you after that first session about how you personally felt about the speech? You seemed to hesitate to say anything; but then when you got the results off those cards, you suddenly were alive with compliments. Why didn't you take a chance before you saw the cards and lay out your feelings and evaluations? I really wanted to know how you felt."

He waited a long moment before replying; and then, in what must have been a difficult time of self-revelation he said, "Do you know how hard it is to realize that you don't have an opinion of your own anymore? I found out early in my job that if I wanted to get ahead I had to be careful not to cross swords with the boss, or buck company policy or give opinions about anything. I found out that the best way to get along and not make a lot of mistakes was just to become a mirror with no opinions of my own."

If you are used to couching everything you say in protective terms for one reason or the other, you may discover that same caution creeping into your speeches. Unconsciously you may be making a way out of any statement. Persuasive speakers take a chance on exposing their views and ideas; and, hardest of all, they assume the full responsibility for them. The audience needs to feel that they are hearing your views and feelings if they are to trust you.

Sometimes, in being called on to speak for a company to its employees, I sense a little tension in my being there. What is happening is that the employees are wondering if I have been hired by the home office to "do a number on them." The approach that I use in these situations that is both sincere and in the best interest of the company, is to challenge that unspoken feeling with an assertion of my own sincerity as a speaker:

"I know you are probably wondering why I am here. Let me assure you I have not come as a mouth of the company. They have not hired me to lay something on you. In fact, I have appreciated the fact that they have let me feel free to share my thoughts and feelings with you."

This is a simple illustration of how to handle opposition from an audience by using the power of sincerity. A full discussion will conclude this chapter later.

Attaching Yourself To Your Message With Strong Personal Ties: Building sincerity with your audience is the process of showing them that what they see is what they get. The most effective way of accomplishing this is by sharing personal experiences and events that show a "piece" of you. An audience is drawn to a speaker when you can open up and invite them to take a look for themselves at the kind of person you are.

As noted, we sometimes have a problem with this because we are exposed in a vulnerable and defenseless way. Hesitancy on our part can result for many reasons:

1. *Our Conditioning From Childhood:* For many reasons we sometimes find ourselves unable to "open up" to an audience. Some have been raised by parents who have stressed "not hanging out their dirty laundry" in public. That's good advice. The only problem is that it's not far from "dirty laundry" to "any laundry." If a child is conditioned to keep things about himself private and out of public view, there will be resistance to any exposure of any personal feelings or views.

Some people are described as keeping everything inside. Whatever the reason, whether it was growing up as an only child with no one to share thoughts and feelings with, or a fear of speaking to parents, they will have difficulty in suddenly being called upon to fling open the doors to their private experiences. If they have a problem relating at this level to those closest to them like their mates, it's no wonder they have considerable difficulty opening up to an audience filled with strangers.

2. The most telling reason most people have a problem in sharing personal experiences about themselves is what we have come to call a *fear of rejection,* the uneasy feeling that if we do reveal "pieces" of our real self, people will not like what they see and will refuse to accept us.

We have been taught to be careful with our feelings and not to "cast our pearls before swine," which is a way of saying, "Be careful how you expose the deepest and most sensitive areas of your life. When you do, you leave yourself open to having people root around in them with very little sensitivity to what they mean to you."

This is of course a real danger in any self-expression, that someone might not understand, or that someone might even laugh at you, but this danger is inherent in the nature of Charis-magic power. There's an old investment law that says "the bigger profits come with the bigger risks." That is true here. The real power in speaking comes as a result of investing the most potentially powerful material—your own personal experiences and feelings. No pains—no gains; no risk—little power.

The *fear of rejection* can only hurt us if we have some basic insecurities about ourselves as worthy persons. If our self-image is in trouble and we have a problem relating to others, we will have considerable difficulty in expressing openness. If, on the other hand, we have a healthy self-love and feel good about who we are and our worth as persons, we can share a piece of ourselves and let it fall where it may. We will not be at the mercy of the others' evaluation of our worth, but can express our feelings and walk away secure in who we are regardless of how others react to us.

On the other side of the coin, a word of caution: If you are the kind of person who has little problem expressing yourself or pouring out your feelings to an audience, remember that there are some in that audience who will have a problem with you. Even as it is difficult for some to express feelings, there are those who have a problem being on the receiving end. If you have strong emotional content, there will be times and occasions when the audience will barely be able to handle it, so walk carefully and try to measure the capacity of your audience for the kinds of things that matter.

As I've indicated, the greatest source of material to relate sincerely with an audience is to be found in our own personal experiences. In Chapter 10 of this book I will be giving you some help on how to uncover them, test them for Charis-magic power and incorporate them into your speeches; but all of this will be of little value if you don't take a chance and use them. **Telling It Like It Is:** In a world of "the best," "the greatest," "fantastic," "super," and "colossal," it is refreshing to hear a voice "tell it like it is." One of the greatest statesman of all times, Winston Churchill, rallied the English people during World War War II by offering them only, "blood, toil, tears, and sweat."

One of the definitions of sincere was "a revealing of just what one feels, thinks or sees and no more." A speaker raises his sincerity impact on an audience when he honestly presents a subject as it really is. I remember a sales manager making a presentation of a new product to his sales force: "I want you to go out there and just tell the people what it will do. I don't want any lying. I just want you to show them the label. Read to them what the label promises and then shut up! Tell them and promise them no more. I want them to be able to go home, and use this product, and be able to say, "It does exactly what it says it can do."

I heard one speaker who daringly advertised himself as, "Not the best speaker in the world, but adequate."

I watched another sales manager at a major manufacturing meeting get up in front of a disgruntled sales force and say, "I know we have had problems with this unit. There's no way I can get around that fact; and I know that it has made it hard for you to sell it. You have had to make excuses for it, and your competition has been making hay out of it, and you have had to go uphill to move it. I regret that, but that's the way it is. Now, while our labs are trying to correct the problem, you help me find some ways we can get together on this headache, and solve it for both of us."

In the hours to follow, they shared ideas, and approaches and tried to find solutions, because the sales manager "told it like it was" and didn't try to pretend the problem didn't exist and blame the drop in sales on his sales force.

Admit You Don't Know It All: No one is perfect and no one has perfect knowledge. When we admit that we do not have all the answers we build credibility with our audience. Our sincerity is enhanced by the fact that we are honest about our need and desire to learn more. This is a thin line to walk. You must maintain an attitude of authority (I know what I am talking about), but also make room for sincerity (I know there is more to this subject).

This is a powerful tool to use when you are in an open discussion and someone comes up with a question or comment that you are not prepared to handle adequately. Rather than try to bluff your way through and take the chance of losing your credibility, it is better to respond, "Thank you for your comment. I'm always trying to learn and you have certainly opened up a new possibility to me. Would you mind taking a moment and expanding on that thought. I know we all will profit from it." You are made to look sincere, the person asking the question enjoys the spotlight, and the audience feels they have been treated with respect.

One of the most effective ways to open a discussion is by admitting: "I certainly don't have all the answers, and I have learned so much from so many by their being willing to share with me. I wonder if you would do me the privilege of helping me to grow and participate in this time of discussion."

Admitting that you don't know it all is a powerfully disarming technique. You will be introduced to a form of it in our discussion on handling hostile audiences. In essence it gives away a little bit of authority in order to gain a lot of sincerity and credibility: a more than fair exchange under any conditions.

Go After Personal Involvement With Your Audience: Your sincerity with an audience is enhanced if they find out you have made a real effort to understand them and what they are doing for a living. Before speaking to a national hair products company, I asked that they send me samples of their shampoos and conditioners so I could say, "I've tried them for myself . . ." When preparing for a seminar with a major construction-firm that specialized in massive water and fluid tanks, I visited one of the sites and had a personal tour and explanation of the procedure. I was able to say, "While spending the day on your Tampa project, I learned some fascinating things about your work . . ."

To prepare for a series of seminars around the state for the employees of Florida Gas Company, I spent a day interviewing a sampling of their staff and workers to be able to relate my material to their specific needs. People sense your sincerity when you "go the extra mile" to prepare for them. They know you would not be knocking yourself out and making the extra effort if you didn't have a sense of personal responsibility to bring them your best.

Next time you are invited to speak, ask yourself what you can do, or where you can go, or to whom you can speak to show you are and want to be personally involved with your audience.

HOW TO DEAL WITH A HOSTILE AUDIENCE

At times you might suddenly find yourself the spokesman for a view that is unpopular or controversial. Your audience may be antagonistic or defensive; and in some cases, even hostile. Of all the situations a speaker can be in, this one offers the most personal risk. At the same time, this situation also opens the door to test the claims of Charis-magic power. If you can get through and touch an audience under these conditions, you have truly demonstrated power.

I have placed the subject of hostile audiences and how to handle them in this chapter because, of all the assurances needed to build trust, the one called sincerity is the most critical in dealing with them. Whatever else is said or done, the audience must feel that you mean what you say. If that note is missing or off pitch the whole situation crumbles.

Certainly you need to be friendly (non-threatening), knowledgeable and show you care; but none of this matters if your audience is not convinced you are sincere.

Here are some guidelines to help in dealing with a hostile or antagonistic audience. I don't promise that using them will win the crowd over; but these techniques will give your arguments a fair hearing and win you some personal respect in the process.

1. Preparing Yourself: Don't take it personally! When preparing to meet a hostile audience, separate your ego from the issues. "Sticks and stones may break your bones but words will never harm you," unless you let them! Prepare yourself mentally before the meeting takes place to "keep your cool" and not react to some personal attack.

In the days of the old West, when a man got out of hand in the local saloon, one of his lines of defense was that it was the whiskey talking. In heated situations, people say and do things they might not under normal stress. Don't take it personally, and don't waste your energy defending yourself. The issue in these meetings is the issue. Repeat it and reinforce yourself with it; *the issue is the issue!*

Utilize your strength and energy in presenting your arguments and blunting the edge of the opposition's, not in protecting your ego.

2. Study the Issues Carefully: "My mind is made up, don't bother me with the facts," might be a cute saying but don't try it with a hostile audience. Study the issues carefully and thoroughly. Clarify them in your mind. Get the facts and be prepared to back them up with sound and reasonable answers.

Determine what are the main points under contention and decide which are critical to your case and which ones you can give away. Concentrate on these issues so you won't be tempted to chase rabbits.

Research and understand the opposition's views and be prepared to deal with them in a sympathetic manner. Remember that they are special to many in the audience. If you mangle them in your treatment of them with unfair accusations and faulty interpretations, you will lose any chance of appearing as a reasonable and fair person.

Out of all your study and research, distill what you consider to be the "heart issues." List them. Prepare a defense for each one of them and then go into the arena of creative imagining with them. See yourself making the point to the audience and then asking for any questions or discussion. Listen to the opposition and defend each point against their arguments with sound and reasonable responses. When you find yourself treed by a question from your practice audience, make a note of it and go on with the debate.

Later, take your notes and work on the areas that you exposed as possible areas of weakness or areas you need more information about. You will be amazed to discover how much surer you will be at the actual meeting once you have faced all the possible questions in the arena of your imagination.

3. How To Relate To a Hostile Audience: In this section I want to discuss certain procedural techniques in handling your audience. These do not involve the actual content of your speech as much as the atmosphere in which you deliver it.

A. Appear as Non-Threatening: We have spent a whole chapter discussing wrapping strength in a friendly image. Now, a smile and a handshake are not going to turn an aggressive crowd around, but certain assurances will take the edge off their concern about you as a threat. Foremost, take the focus off them personally and place it on the issues. If they feel that your remarks are aimed at them, they will become defensive; but if you clarify from the beginning that the matters under consideration are at stake, you will keep them listening:

"You all have a right to feel the way you do. That's what it means to be a part of this country. I'm not any different from you. I want the best for my family and want to enjoy the good things of life, but once in a while people come into disagreement on issues. It is the issues I am here to talk about. I appreciate the privilege you have given me and even as I state my case, I respect your right to your viewpoint."

I heard an advocate in a debate over a new county sewer system turn to his opponents in the middle of a heated moment and say, "It's a shame we had to get so heated up over a sewer line. I'll be glad when this thing is over so we can go back to enjoying our friendships again!" He made a distinction between the issues and the people.

B. Get Your Sincerity Out Front: If there is ever a time you must communicate to an audience that you are a person who means what he says, this is it. From the very moment you reach the platform you need to establish that you stand behind what you have to say: you are expressing your own feelings. "You might not agree with me. I can understand that, but I want you to know I'm going to be honest and straightforward about how I feel and where I stand. I believe you are the kind of people who would want it that way."

Another approach I heard involved a woman who was advocating sex education in the school system: "You know, I could wish this issue never came up. My life was so much simpler before I found myself in the middle of all this controversy. I could wish that young people didn't find themselves in the quandary of unwanted pregnancies and frightening abortions, but they do. I could wish that I could take you inside my mind and let you see that there is no evil intent, only a desire to help, but I can't. All I can say is I find myself where I didn't expect to be, fighting for a cause I didn't ask to get into, hoping that, whatever else you believe about me, you will believe that I am sincerely searching for the answers that will touch some young lives."

Get your sincerity out front. Tell the audience exactly how you feel about the situation, but then be ready to back it up with cold facts and reasonable answers.

C. *Use Straight Talk:* An antagonistic audience is just waiting for you to come up with some loaded material that is slanted in your favor. They are just waiting to hear you spout it so they can say, "You must think we are a bunch of dummies. Who in his right mind would buy that distorted interpretation?"

Use simple and clear language. State the issues in such a way that there can be no misunderstanding. Don't exaggerate and don't intimidate. Just describe the situation the way it is. So many speakers have lost their credibility by crying "wolf." They are always making such claims as, "Unless this regulation is passed, the whole economy of the nation will crumble!" "Oh, come on! Who's going to believe that? You mean to say that the whole economy of America is teetering on the brink of disaster and we can stop it by just passing this little old regulation?"

Audiences have been surviving scare tactics like this for years. They certainly aren't going to be impressed when you drag them up again in order to try and get your point across. Tell it like it is!

4. Preparing the Content Of Your Speech: The best defense is a good offense. If you incorporate answers to questions that are going to be asked in your speech, and if you anticipate the mood of your audience, you can "pull the teeth of the opposition." By this I mean you can render many of their arguments harmless by the way you anticipate them and deal with them. It's better to meet the "enemy" on your ground. This is done in careful speech preparation.

A. Deal With Tough Questions: If you want to beat the audience to the punch, bring up tough criticisms of your position during the course of your speech. Show not only a willingness, but a desire to deal with them and answer them. If these were the main arguments of your opposition, you have in effect "pulled their teeth." They can't hurt you with these issues as much as they had planned. The shock value is gone and you certainly won't be shown to be ignorant of the arguments.

I witnessed one of the most profound examples of this principle in action when I attended a lecture at the University of North Carolina. The noted professor of philosophy speaking that evening was a guest at a symposium of philosophic studies. At the end of his prepared remarks he opened the floor for questions. One young and eager philosophy student immediately asked him, "Is it true that you have a personal belief in God?"

To almost everyone's amazement and without the usual academic fanfare the professor answered simply, "Yes, I do."

The young student was obviously delighted with the situation and started, "I can't understand how a man of your stature and education can believe in a God?"

"Well," he answered graciously, "if you can show me a better alternative, I'll be ready to make a change."

The young student proceeded to give a ten-minute summary of arguments against the existence of God and for an atheistic position. When he concluded, the room was silent, waiting for the professor's response. "I must admit your arguments are good. They are well-structured and well thought out. I find only one problem . . . you are an amateur atheist."

"Amateur?"

"Yes; you see there are many other and better arguments for your position." He then proceeded to give a discourse on atheism that was remarkably thorough and completely sound academically. When he finished, he added a final word.

"Now that we've had an opportunity to hear your position, I hope you will allow me the same opportunity to speak for a few moments on the meaning of a mature faith."

When you anticipate the problem areas and deal with them on your own terms, you are a long way down the road of "pulling the teeth" of the opposition.

B. *Show You Are Reasonable:* Show your audience that you understand there are two sides to the issues. Use phrases that show you have not closed your mind to their position: "I can understand how you would come to that conclusion . . ." "That argument certainly makes sense if you are looking at it from your perspective . . ." You are certainly entitled to feel the way you do about this situation . . ."

Show a knowledge of other viewpoints. Incorporate your understanding of those viewpoints into your remarks. If you really want to add the power of credibility, quote directly from the opposition's sources: "While reading through your magazine, I noticed an article that has to do with the subject tonight. In this article the writer has said that . . ."

As a reasonable person, be willing to concede minor points to the opposition. In the section on preparation, I mentioned that you need to decide which issues can be given away. You will discover that giving in on some minor issues might be the very leverage you need to win the big ones.

Several years ago I attended a zoning meeting because my land was affected by the requested change. A church was asking that ten acres of land that they had purchased be rezoned for "general church purposes" and then they had listed items such as parking, recreation, educational facilities, day care center, retirement center.

Some of the neighborhood had become quite vocal in their opposition and wanted to prevent the rezoning procedure from going through. The hearing before the county commissioners became pretty heated and slowly the issue began to revolve around the proposed retirement center that the zoning change would allow.

A flood of arguments came pouring out from the neighbors in opposition to the idea. In the middle of the heat, the minister of the church asked to speak:

"Since the retirement center is such an issue, we would be willing to strike it from the petition." The room grew very silent. The chairman of the commissioners said, "That seems fair enough," and the zoning change was passed.

Afterwards, I asked the minister how deleting the retirement center would affect his building program. "Oh, no problem. You see we had no plans for a retirement center. In fact, the land is not suited for any heavy construction. It was little enough to give away to get all we got in the process."

Be willing to concede small points. You might find this will give you the leverage you need to win the big ones.

5. Answering Questions From The Floor: This is what your "creative imagining" was preparing you for—the moment of truth when your opposition gets to question you directly. Simple points: "keep your cool." "Don't take any questions personally," and "don't chase rabbits." Stay with the central issues that you have come to debate.

In concluding this section on "How To Deal With a Hostile Audience," I'm reminded of the fact that there really isn't much of a challenge in speaking to an audience that is sympathetic to your views, but nothing beats going up against an audience that is primarily against you at the start and coming away with a rousing round of applause.

A MOMENT OF REVIEW

Charis-magic power is the result of the speaker's ability to build a relationship of trust with his audience. This trust zone depends on the speaker's ability to give certain assurances about himself to his audience. We have looked at three of these: the speaker is *friendly, knowledgeable* and *sincere*. In the next chapter, we will approach the fourth of these assurances—the speaker is *caring*.

 Seven

How To
Express Your Feelings
With
Charis-Magic Results

Every psychologist knows the principle. In fact, in recent years, many of them have changed their whole approach to therapy as a result of taking it seriously:

"If you are going to reach out and touch another human life and help heal someone's pain, you can't do it by sitting back in a leather chair and looking down your objective nose. You must get involved! Show emotion! Let the patient see that you care; because unless you are able to show your caring, the words of cure, the remedy will not be accepted or believed!"

If Charis-magic power is going to be a reality for you as a public speaker, you will need to come to grips with the assurance called caring. Most simply defined, caring is the "vibe" or impression that you give your audience that convinces them you are concerned about their welfare. If sincerity looks primarily to the relationship of the speaker to his message, "I mean what I say," then caring looks primarily at the relationship of the speaker to his audience, "I want the best for you."

PEOPLE KEEP FEELING THE HOOKS

People, and audiences as well, have a need to feel that you are interested and concerned about them as individuals, not merely as pawns to be manipulated. People are very weary of having hooks put in them and feet wiped on them. They are wary of any relationship where they are apparently going to be used for selfish ends, to satisfy the intents of the other.

An audience is suspicious of any speaker who comes on as though he were going to use them for his own purposes, "like chickens to be plucked!" Just saying you care will not make it so. Audiences have been bombarded by claims of caring. They have been told that out there in this cruel world someone really cares about their weight, their bust sizes, their teeth, their egos, you name it, and for $9.95 and a coupon they have been promised that all their problems can be cleared up—from acne to acrophobia.

You are going to have to do a real selling job to show you are not just giving them another set of idle and inoperative promises; that when you say "I care about you as a person," you are honestly concerned that the listener goes away from you in better shape than he was when he came to you.

DEALING WITH EMOTIONALISM

I want to make a careful distinction between showing an audience how much you care and emotionalism, the constant arousing of an emotional state. I am not advocating that you go to the podium looking to "cry your eyes out" as a mark of your caring. Some speakers I have met can turn their tears on like a water faucet the minute they are in the spotlight. They treat the podium as though it were a psychiatrist's couch where they can go and have an emotional catharsis. As far as they are concerned, the audience is a spectator to their award-winning performances.

Arriving late for a meeting in Houston, I rushed to the hotel where I was speaking in time to be confronted by the previous speaker, a woman who just "loved" everybody. She was sorry that I had missed hearing her speak and then made a remark that in her mind indicated the depth of her performance: "I got so involved in my message that I cried three times!"

My caution about emotionalism does not preclude the possibility that in some high moment of personal disclosure you will not feel some emotional impact on you. What I am dealing with here is a style of speaking before audiences. Some speakers are reminiscent of the good old days of movie-making when the heroine would weep her heart out by gently dabbing her face with a handkerchief soaked in onion juice.

Strong showing of emotion, to be powerful and effective, must be in harmony with the content of the message and the personality of the speaker. Some emotional "bits" of speakers are so well-practiced and grooved that they come off as phony as a laugh track on an old television program. They just seem inappropriate for the situation. The response is not warranted by the materials. Emotional content in speeches, caring about people and expressing that caring, must be consistent with your total personality if it is to come off as authentic and genuine. Then you have power!

Now, I'm aware that the majority of speakers do not have a problem with emotionalism. In fact, if anything, they have probably overreacted to it and the problem is showing emotion of any kind.

How can you show that your caring and your emotions are genuine and not manufactured for the occasion? During the course of this chapter, I will share some guidelines with you that will be of help in leading you through a maze of possible misunderstanding to Charis-magic power.

Granted that up to this point I have asked you to be open,

natural, non-aggressive, knowledgeable and sincere. Now to all that add one more—caring.

HOW TO EXPRESS YOURSELF AS A CARING PERSON

Show a Caring Involvement With Your Message: Here again you are confronted by the powerful principle I outlined in the last chapter and have advocated throughout this book, "Charis-magic power depends on your ability to put your life on the line!" The audience wants to know that you have a personal relationship with your message and that it just isn't some "sugar stick" you go around feeding different groups.

They want to feel that you care about the content of your message and that you have poured something of the kind of person you are into it. If they do not feel this is the case, they will begin to question and ask: "How can he say he cares about me when he doesn't even care about what he's talking about?"

As a speaker who is looking for power, you are called on to line up your life with the contents of your message. One of the most dramatic yet quiet moments I have ever witnessed of this quality occurred several years ago at a Rotary Club annual banquet.

Before I was to speak, the president of the club introduced a Rotarian who was going to serve as chairman of their committee to raise funds for cancer research, one of the major projects of the club for that coming year. He came to the platform and graciously accepted his appointment and then added:

"Many of you are probably wondering why I got myself all tied up with this project, knowing all the other things I've got my fingers in. Well, the reason is really very simple. For the past five years I've been fighting a personal battle against cancer; and now I'm going to fight not only for my life, but for the lives of others as well."

Now, your encounters with your audiences may not have this dramatic quality, but the principle is the same. Somehow you need to wrap up the content of your message "bits and pieces" of yourself that demonstrate you are a genuine and caring person.

I heard an executive address the Board of Directors right after they had elected him as president of the company: "You all know that this business was started by my father, and I am not fool enough to forget the guiding genius he brought to it during those early days. Now you have asked me to continue in the tradition of strong leadership that has come down the line—a challenging order for any man. I'm not sure I can measure up to his intuitive skills, but I am sure I will do everything in my power to match his great pride and caring spirit for this company."

This executive translated his response to the board by giving them something of himself. "Bits and pieces" were strewn throughout his speech, welding it together with a sense of sincerity and personal involvement.

Of all the characters in American history I have always been fascinated by Patrick Henry. It was said of him, by a man who had heard many of his speeches that, "He is by far the most powerful speaker I have ever heard. Every word he says not only engages but commands attention."

I have read many of of his speeches and tried to analyze them to distill whatever secret I could from the pages, and I have come to at least a part of the conclusion of the source of his great power as a speaker. Note these tremendously moving lines delivered in 1775 before the Virginia Provincial Convention:

"Gentlemen may cry, Peace, Peace! – but there is no peace. The war is already begun . . . Is life so dear, or peace so sweet, as to be purchased at the price of chains and slavery? Forbid it, Almighty God! I know not what course others may take; but as for me, give me liberty or give me death!"

All of Henry's writings are riddled with "bits and pieces" of himself. You feel the vitality of commitment in his words. You don't have to guess about the genuineness of his spirit. You know he cares about what he is talking about. He has lain his life on the line.

Share Bits and Pieces of Yourself Throughout Your Speech:
What follows are some practical techniques that you can use to drop "bits and pieces" of the kind of person you are throughout your speech, the prime objective being to build the assurance that you are a caring person.

Use the Introduction: Earlier in the book I stated that the prime purpose of your Introduction was to establish your authority to speak on the subject. I also mentioned that there are some support uses of the Introduction and here is an example. You might want to mention some activity or position that indicates your role as a caring person: "serving as chairman of the United Heart Fund," "on the executive committee of the YMCA," "recently given the Mayor's Award for his outstanding contribution to community pride."

Say that You Care: At first my suggestion that you just say you care might sound a little crass, but it doesn't have to be. To say "I care" is a disclosure of yourself in clear and simple language that has profound impact. Let the words come naturally and use them to appropriately introduce a matter that concerns you:

"*I care* very much what happens to my town and the lakes that have made it so beautiful through the years," "*I care* about what's happening to my children. *I care* about the quality of education they are getting and the kind of world they are facing and the pressures and expectations that are put on them. *I care!*"

It's a powerful phrase and when used honestly has a powerful impact on those listening. Say it with your lips. Work it into your material. Take an index card and write on it in bold letters, "I CARE." Put it in front of you while you are preparing your speech and experiment with its power.

Take an ordinary sentence like, "Our town has a rising crime rate," and give it a touch of personal power by adding the phrase, "*I care* that our town has a rising crime rate!" Immediately you are thrown into the situation in a personal way. A bit of you is now lodged in the sentence and power is born.

Tell A Story that Shows You Care: Another way to put a "piece" of you into your speech is to tell a story that shows you as a caring person. The key to doing this in good taste is to put the story in what I call a casual framework. The story of caring is told simply as a backdrop for telling another story. For instance, in one of my speeches I may be dealing with the idea of how some people start living without expectations:

"It's sad, sad to find out that you have no more dreams, no

more challenges, no more desire to reach for the stars. So many are dead! Just waiting to be buried. Growing days are over. All that's left is withering away and dying!

"Near my home in Orlando we have a special hospital that cares for specially handicapped and retarded from all over the south. Each year my family takes them on as our Christmas project. For weeks in advance we find gifts—a toy for a child, a little portable radio for a man, a brush and comb for a lady.

"You can never leave there without feeling a little more thankful that you can walk and breathe deep of life. Of all the sights that bombard your mind and eyes, the most poignant is to see a grown man's body with the mind of a child in it. Somewhere along the way in the mystery of the miracle of life, the mind quit growing . . . Sad, almost as sad as a man who no longer feels a desire to be more, to experience more, to stretch for another adventure in the infinite possibilities of tomorrow."

The primary story was about growing and stretching, but it was framed in a setting that said "he is a caring person." Many of you will feel more comfortable with this technique than with simply telling a story about you and your family helping retarded children.

Without the casual framework, the story might come off as blowing your horn or as simply a story you have told to impress others, but your heart wasn't in it. We must all walk carefully here. There is nothing quite as repugnant as feeling that someone has used the pain of another to advance his own sense of worth.

Use Introductory Phrases: This is basically the same technique I was showing you in dealing with how to establish your authority as a speaker. With this skill you can drop "bits and pieces" of your caring image all through the speech with quick, short jabs; "We had just returned from working all night on the telethon for C.P. when . . ." "I was standing there in the freezing cold trying to sell Christmas trees for the Boy's Club when along came this man with a huge dog . . ." "I had just finished going all over my neighborhood trying to find my neighbor's missing lawn mower when the phone rang and . . ."

Locate incidents, experiences, events, moments in your

life that are genuine and warm examples of caring and work them into your content. They might appear as introductory phrases or within the casual framework of another story, but let them flow. Like a mighty river let them come down in the guise of casual offhand remarks, and see them turn the dynamo that generates Charis-magic power.

Developing Empathy With Your Audience: Empathy is your ability to sense how another person feels or thinks. When your audiences sense that you understand them, that you have the capacity to get inside them, they will find it easier to believe that you really care about them.

Developing empathy is a matter of conditioning yourself to relive certain past experience so you can relate to what others are going through now. To be able to say, "I understand" or "I know what you are feeling" builds strong rapport and trust with your audience.

Last year I was invited to speak at the Annual Meeting of the Chamber of Commerce of a small mining community in West Virginia. The miners had been on strike for some time and the community was beginning to feel the pressure. The local merchants were losing business and their books were already backlogged with the credit charges of the people who were out of work.

The winter had been difficult and left them with their funds and resources exhausted. Discouragement and a feeling of gloom was in the air, especially since there was no immediate prospect that the strike would end. When I got up to speak that night, I shared a few private thoughts with the audience:

"I think I know a little bit of what you are going through. I was raised in Brooklyn, New York, the son of immigrants, during the great depression of the thirties. Shortly after I was born, my father died and my mother took in sewing and worked in a little dress shop doing alterations to try and hold us together as a family.

"There were four of us children and many days our meal was a day-old sandwich we bought for a nickel from a bakery around the corner who made them for the factory workers. We all did what we could. I even resorted to singing on the street corners for a few pennies a day, but we did what we could; and somehow we held together. And we came to love and appreciate each other more because of it.

My words for you tonight, "Good News in the Middle of Hard Times."

When a speaker has a high degree of empathy and he is able to read the feelings of his audience, he will develop a strong bond with them. Without this empathy a speaker becomes insensitive to his audience; and an insensitive speaker is headed for difficulty in building rapport and trust.

The insensitive speaker is usually marked by the tendency to "serve up the same hash" regardless of the situation or the nature of the audience. I was speaking at a September Days Club meeting in Richmond, Virginia. The audience was made up of a great fellowship of retired people who traveled all over the United States enjoying special activities and programs planned for them.

As part of this particular program, they had hired a performing group to come in and present a song and dance routine for the over six hundred people gathered at the banquet. Obviously, they had not done their homework and "tuned in" to the kind of people attending.

They sang a lot of songs from contemporary Broadway shows that nobody knew. Their jokes were in bad taste and dealt with subjects of little interest to the audience. They may have thought they were charming and cute but as the program wore on it became evident that they had lost the audience. In fact, or in frustration, the president of the club actually stood up in the middle of one of the songs, thanked them and proceeded to introduce me. As I came to the podium, I could still hear the voice of one of the singers yelling out, "But we're not through yet!" He may not have known it then, but he was!

They came to do "their thing." If they had been sensitive to the needs and feelings of the audience, they would still be getting invitations to return again.

Empathy is one of the most powerful tools in the kit of the persuasive speaker; this ability to read into and feel with your audience; this sensitivity to "tune in" to their mood and adjust your material to meet it. Sometimes the people are tired; time to lighten up. Sometimes they are discouraged; time to give them a hand. Sometimes they are elated and excited; time to give them a chance to let off some steam.

Researching Your Audiences: The speaker who just plods through the same old material has little chance of experiencing Charis-magic power. The audience can sense when a speaker is just going through the motions. Note, I am not saying that repeating the same material is in itself a mark that the speaker is not sensitive to his audiences. I know many persuasive speakers who carry the same basic message with them wherever they go. The difference is in what you do with the material; whether you adjust, change, fine tune it to meet the needs of your audience, or whether you just hang it out there to dry.

Work at developing empathy. Put yourself in the place of your audience. Try to feel as they feel and think as they think. Put yourself in their shoes and feel the pressure of a long day of work sessions, or sense the anticipation for an evening of fun, or smell the tension in the air. Find the audience's expectations. Ask yourself what kind of speaker you would like to listen to at a time like this. What would be your expectations?

One of the hardest times I have ever had at a meeting was in New Orleans. Because of a long plane delay, I arrived late and had little time to "feel out" my audience. When I got up to speak that night, nothing seemed to happen. No matter how I tried, I couldn't seem to find the temperature of my audience. I felt that my material was just dying on the vine. No matter what I tried there was very little response. I closed to polite applause.

After the meeting, as I was leaving, I happened to overhear a couple speaking and heard the man say, "He wasn't very funny, was he?" Noticing a brochure on the table I picked it up and found the key to my problem. Someone had decided to spice the banquet up and cast me in a new role. "Come and hear Dick Milham, one of America's funniest men. He will have you rolling in the aisle."

No wonder I was out of tune with my audience. They were expecting a clown. This is a rare instance when the damage was done from the outside, but it serves as an example of how powerless we become if we are not sensitive to the audience's expectations and needs.

The next time you are invited to speak, ask some questions about the audience: Who will be there, men, women, both? Why are they coming, to receive an award, to install new officers, to just have a good time? What kind of work do they do, mechanics, clerks, engineers, farmers? Research that audience. Try to get as much information as you can to get a profile of the kind of people you will be talking to, and then ask yourself, "What would I expect the speaker to talk on for an occasion like this?"

Putting Your Motives Out Front: Another way of assuring your audience that you are a caring person is by exposing your motives for being there to speak. In the next chapter I will deal with how to relate your speech to some benefit for your audience, but at this point I simply want to show that a caring motive has power to build rapport and trust with them.

Obviously, one of the questions that is running through the mind of the audience is why you are there. I've said that this can be one of the sources of audience resistance. If they feel you are a threat, they will become defensive and pull into their psychological shells; but suppose you can convince them that your reason for coming is because you care about them. Suppose you can show them that your motive is simply a desire to reach them and help them in some way?

Again, using the casual framework, you might expose your motive and show it to be one that is not out to hurt them. Tell a story that will show you in a caring framework.

Several years ago I was asked to speak to over eight thousand young people in Raleigh, North Carolina. While facing the problem of how I was going to relate to them to get my message across, I remembered an incident that had happened to me in that town a few months earlier. I opened my session by sharing the incident and making a few remarks about it:

"You're probably wondering who I am and what I am and what I am doing here. I can understand that. I would be too. Let me share a story with you that might help you to understand me a little better, and strangely enough, it happened right on this same platform six months ago.

"I had come to Raleigh to speak at the FHA State Convention. What an exciting bunch of kids they were, almost as turned on to life as you. I got into town early to have lunch with some good friends over in Durham. I had a great meal and then my friend turned on the television to catch the early afternoon news.

"The reporter was in Vietnam and was telling about an attempt to evacuate a group of orphan children from an area being run over by the enemy. The plane crashed on takeoff killing over forty of the children. I remember turning to my friend and saying something like, "Isn't that a shame?" You know, the kind of thing you say when you don't know what to say.

"I drove down here to Raleigh to speak, just as I'm doing tonight, and when I finished I had a phone call waiting for me. My friend was on the line and he said, "Dick, do you remember that news story about the plane crash and the children? My brother was on that plane."

"When I got to his house he had pieced together what had happened. His brother had been stationed in the area and loved to spend time with the children in the orphanage. He gave them all the time he could spare and when he heard about the evacuation, he volunteered to help get them out. When they found his body he had a child in each arm, and when we asked why he did it, all we could come up with was, *he cared!*

"Now, I can't stand up here and tell you I'd die for you. I really don't know and I guess none of us would really know unless the time came when we had to do it; but I can tell you that I really care about you, each and every one of you, and I've come to share some thoughts that might make your lives a little fuller and happier."

Tell a story, apply it, expose your motives, discover power.

Show You Have The Capacity to Feel and Be Moved: Audiences have a hard time warming up to a speaker who gives the impression that his feelings are tucked away in a freezer for safekeeping. The audience wants to feel that you are human, just as they are. They want to sense that you are vulnerable and capable of being moved and touched by the feelings and situations of others.

For you to be able to say "I care" means, in their minds, that you must also be able to say "I feel." The audience is looking for more than intellectural appraisals based on the latest statistics; they want to know how you feel. They don't want some lip service to the effect that "there are thousands suffering from malnutrition in America." They want to know how this information affects you. They want to hear you say, "As a father, I think I can feel what it would be like to put my children to bed hungry every night, yet thousands do!"

To be a persuasive speaker, you need to find "bits and pieces" in your emotional life and share them with your audience so they can sense that you feel with them. This is more than telling a story about taking gifts to retarded children; this is describing the impact of that experience and how it hit you "in the gut." The purpose of this approach in speaking to your audience is to show them through a personal illustration that you can be touched as a person.

Again, go back to your experiences and find an event that has moved you and look to see how you can use it in your speech. Let vitality flow into it. Use descriptive words that tell how you feel. Let the illustration serve as a showcase for your emotions. Show that you can get angry, sad, frustrated, weary. Let it declare your emotional involvement with life. The audience is looking for someone who understands them; someone just like them who feels with them, laughs with them, hurts with them.

Feeling Good About Feeling: Earlier in this chapter I stated that the problem with most speakers is not emotionalism but probably an overreaction to emotion of any kind in their speeches.

We have been so conditioned, especially men, to hide our feelings: "You're a big boy now, and big boys don't cry," "Shame on you, what would the neighbors think if they saw you crying?" "Wipe that smile off your face," "A real man doesn't cry, only girls cry."

No wonder so many have difficulty letting their emotions flow naturally to their audience. We have come to equate the showing of *any* emotion in public as a sign of weakness.

"Be strong and don't cry" has been the conditioning, and because of this we have lost tremendous power in reaching others just like us who feel, hurt, laugh, get discouraged and "do dumb things." The man, the speaker, the human being who can own his own emotions and openly share his feelings with others has great drawing power. He is like a magnetic field that attracts people to himself with "I feel just like you do."

When this rapport is established with the audience and they are caught up in it, then the words "I care" take on Charis-magic power. Now these words are backed up with flesh and blood capable of feeling. The podium is no place for Platonic relationships. In the words of the psychologist, "If you are going to reach out and touch another human . . . show emotion!"

In preparing your speech, find an expression or experience of your life that is filled with emotional content and make some statement of the kind of feeling person you are through it. You can set it in the casual framework while telling another story. I want to share an example of this with you, but first a word of caution about this illustration. Here is an example of strong emotional involvement; but it is not intended to be a model. In selecting a story to tell, the key is not finding one with dramatic feelings, but honest feelings.

In this story, the point I was trying to make had to do with persistence, staying with it no matter what the odds; but note the emotional impact of what I tried to say about myself as a feeling person.

"Last year I was invited to speak at the high school graduation in my home town. The principal was a long time friend and we had finally managed to work it out. You know, there's something very warm and nostalgic about high school graduations. Every time I go to one I get soft inside and remember my own. All the excitement, the nervous laughter, the bittersweet ache realizing you might never see each other again.

"That's what it was like at this graduation. Seems like nothing changes. As is the custom, they put me on first to speak. I felt I did pretty well and then settled back for the giving out of the diplomas. Name after name. I thought it would go on forever. I could hardly keep my eyes open as the afternoon dragged on, and then it happened. A name was called and a quiet hush fell over the whole crowd; and then I saw her, about halfway up the aisle. Unlike the others, she had stayed in her seat until her name was called.

"I watched her as she seemed to struggle to get to her feet and then I watched as she moved into the aisle and started to come forward. She was slightly teetering, slightly swaying.

"The principal leaned over to me and said, 'She's been in a wheelchair all the time she's been in high school; an automobile accident. The students have helped her get around all these years.'

'But she's walking,' I said.

"Then he told me, 'Yes, for all these years she's been fighting, struggling, exercising, praying that on the day of her graduation she would be able to walk down the aisle on her own.'

"I watched her, fascinated. I saw the slight lurches of her body and saw her grab control again. At every step I found myself pulling with her, and soon I felt my throat choking up and my eyes beginning to mist.

"When she finally got to the front, when she reached out for her diploma, when that whole crowd of stunned teenagers came to their feet cheering, my tears joined their tears.

"What courage! What determination! What persistence!"

Do not be afraid to show that you have the capacity to feel and be moved. Honest emotions are a floodgate to Charis-magic power.

An Exercise In Expressing Yourself: All through these chapters on sincerity and caring (feeling) I have been saying that a speaker needs to deliver these assurances about himself by dropping "bits and pieces" of himself throughout his speech.

This, of course, depends on the speaker's ability to express himself and feel comfortable doing it before his audience. I had the experience, though, of trying to help a man who had an extremely difficult time sharing on a personal level.

His speeches were devoid of any personal illustrations or inputs. His bearing was controlled, his voice almost a monotone, and his eyes and face showed very little expression. He felt comfortable with *knowledge* but not feelings.

I suggested that we begin by getting him to share some "bits and pieces" about himself in a casual framework. To do this we needed to find some experiences that he would feel comfortable in sharing. We went over a lot of possibilities and nothing seemed appropriate until I happened to mention that I did a lot of canoeing in Florida. It was as though I had turned a switch on.

He became very animated, his eyes almost lit up and he started to spill words out in almost a torrent about his love for rafting in white waters on the rivers. He was filled with stories about the dangerous rapids, the rock slides, the swamped rafts, wet clothes and baked beans by a fireside. We had our illustration; nothing dramatic, but filled with real emotions and feelings.

I used his experience in rafting to illustrate the need to be prepared when you are facing unexpected situations: "When you are getting ready to go on a raft through rapids at about twenty-five to thirty miles an hour, you have to be prepared for anything. It could be unexpected high waters, or rock slides or wild animals, but at every turn something unexpected might turn up."

At first, he was a little stiff about sharing his adventures, but slowly he started to warm up to it, and with that came increased animation and vitality in his voice and sparkle in his eyes. He was tapping emotional energy and it was beginning to show.

It wasn't long until I got him to add other personal notes—how they rescued a stranded fawn on an island (*how to win the game through cooperation*), and soon moved to other areas of personal involvement, his work with an organization to help preserve wildlife in its natural habitats. The stories kept coming and the speeches were injected with "bits and pieces."

The last time I heard him, he included in his speech a powerfully moving illustration of his involvement in trying to save the life of an American bald eagle *(spending some time with the things that count)*. It might not look like much on paper, but when he got through with his inputs of personal caring, you could feel the moment.

Find an experience, a moment or event filled with feelings and ease it into your speech, a bit, a piece at a time. Reveal yourself to be a person who cares.

PLOTTING OUR COURSE:

Searching for Charis-magic power requires delving into the force and impact of our emotions. This chapter has given us just a taste of that adventure. In the chapter to follow, we will be dealing with another force, the psychological skill of how to "make an offer that can't be refused" in your speeches.

If the assurances of *friendly, knowledgeable* and *caring* deal primarily with the relationship of the *speaker to his audience,* and if the assurance of *sincerity* deals primarily with the relationship of the *speaker to his message,* then the last of the assurances, *benefits,* has to do primarily with the relationship of the speaker's *message to his audience.*

What, as a speaker, do you offer to your audience in your speech? Can the answer to that question be the final key to the riddle of Charis-Magic power?

 Eight

Applying Charis-Magic To Human Need and Greed

Speaking with Charis-Magic power involves your ability as a speaker to relate your message to certain psychological and social needs of your audience. These needs are a part of the very fiber of human personality and cannot be ignored if you are going to effectively move your audience with persuasive power.

Building trust with your audience requires this, the last of the five assurances, showing them that your message has a benefit or need satisfier for them.

The Five Basic Human Needs:

1. *Survival Need:* "I need to stay alive."

2. *Security Need:* "I need to feel safe from danger and threats."

3. *Social Acceptance Need:* "I need love and a sense of belonging to the group."

4. *Self-Esteem Need:* "I need self-respect and appreciation from others.

5. *Self-Achievement Need:* "I need to reach my full potential and do what I've always wanted to do."

The more effectively a speaker is able to apply his speech content to these needs, the stronger will be his rapport with his audience. The extent to which he fails to show the relevance of his materials to these needs, will determine his lack of Charis-Magic power. He may have good content, delivery and be self-assured, but, unless he speaks to needs, his speech will die in its tracks as far as persuasive power is concerned.

The speech might even be received by the audience as an excellent presentation of information, but the message of this book is how to get an audience to its feet, not how to give them good notes. The objective of our adventure together is not to produce better lecturers, but to empower you to become a persuader!

The message is the power to move people!

Persuasive power demands good content; I have always argued for that. Charis-magic power is not some form of hypnotic cheerleading or gimmick to stir up the emotions, but good content does not assure you of persuasive power. The crux of the matter here is *how the content is applied* to "where the people live." Content without practical application is stripped of its possible power regardless of how enlightening it might be.

UNCOVERING THE BASIC NEEDS
OF YOUR AUDIENCE

An effective application of your message to the needs of your audience might be helped by a closer analysis of these needs:

1. Survival Need: "I need to stay alive."

All people have a basic set of needs that have to do with simply staying alive as a functioning body. These needs have been called the instincts of survival, the need for food, water, shelter, air, sleep, and other factors that keep the breath of life in us.

This is animal level existence. Here is found the drive for life and self-preservation and the theory of the survival of the fittest. If one of these needs is not met, a person can become totally absorbed in pursuing it and trying to satisfy it.

A man wandering in the desert thirsting for water will be totally committed to one thing, finding water. A man who is starving will think of nothing but food and if the hunger becomes intense enough, he will expose himself to danger and in some instances even kill in order to stay alive. These are survival instincts, powerful, driving forces that cling to the preservation of the life of a person.

I recently heard a political leader from a starving country say, "We are not looking for luxuries, we are just asking for bread to stay alive." When a person does not have enough money for survival needs, when he finds he can't pay the rent, or buy food for his family or keep himself warm in the freezing weather, he becomes totally concerned with survival instincts.

If you are speaking to an audience of people who are on a survival level of existence, if they are living hand to mouth or struggling just to stay alive, you need to be aware that they are not interested in pretty philosophies and nebulous promises. They want to know how what you say can be translated into bread to eat.

In my illustration of the coal miners in West Virginia who were on strike and feeling survival pressures, the men called on to speak to them had to talk in terms of what the contract meant for survival, not in terms of their relationship to some great cause. A hungry person is going to cut through all the garbage pretty quickly. He wants to "talk turkey."

Nations have been overthrown by uprisings where the leaders promised food, and those in power kept yelling about tradition.

Point of Application: Can the content of your message be shown to be a benefit or need satisfier for your audience in the area of *survival* need? Will your message provide more food, better shelter, cleaner air, purer water, warmer clothes?

2. Security Need: "I need to feel safe from danger and threats."

The next level of human need is concerned with physical and psychological security. As a person's survival needs are met, a new set of needs rise to claim his attention. He wants to feel unthreatened and live securely.

This need takes the form of several different expressions: He wants protection from physical harm for himself and his family, so he pays to have a police force and a fire department, and a national defense system with armies and weapons. He wants the assurance of good health, so he buys health insurance, and goes on diets, and spends money on tennis and golf, and downs aspirins by the ton, and gets annual checkups.

He wants to feel that his job is secure, so he joins unions, and feathers his nest, and wants tenure; because if his job goes, he's back in the hole of fighting for survival needs. That's the reason if his job security is threatened he becomes very anxious and can even get mean.

If you are speaking to an audience that is concerned about security, you need to "tune in" your message to that level. They may represent an industry that is on the verge of collapse or a business that is going under. Possibly it's a time when people in general are nervous about the economy or the threat of war or international politics. During these times of insecurity, people are looking for words of assurance.

The fear of loss of security has been the big stick in the arguments for increasing military power and allocating more funds to fight crime waves. The fear of loss of health has spurred people to increase exercising, send money for cancer research and give up smoking. The fear of loss of employment has motivated people to go back to school for additional training. All of these examples and many more show the overriding concerns of people who are primarily "tuned in" to security needs.

Point of Application: Can the content of your message be shown to be a benefit or need satisfier for your audience in the area of *security* need? Will your message provide job security, better health, a safer neighborhood, more hospital care, money for retirement, protection for the family?

3. Social Acceptance Need: "I need love and a sense of belonging." As the other needs of survival and security are satisfied, the need for love, affection and a sense of belonging to the group tend to emerge as areas of primary concern. This is what some sociologists have called our "herd instinct," and is reflected in our need for healthy relationships, friendships, professional societies, sororities, civic clubs and the like

Frustration at this level of human need is the source of the most common maladjustments and psychological problems. When these needs for meaningful relationships are short-circuited, a person finds himself in serious emotional trouble. Without the approval of the group, a person has a problem feeling a sense of self-worth. He looks for the validation of his worth by the group's acceptance of him, and if it is not forth-coming, he feels rejected.

This social acceptance need explains the intensity of some people's attempts to impress others. They seek to win the approval of the group by the clothes they wear, the car they drive or the exclusive clubs they belong to. This is the level at which most young people operate in their formative years. They are not too concerned about the problems of survival and security. Mom and Dad are handling those areas. They are free to concentrate on being socially accepted, "one of the gang." Peer pressure is the name of that game.

In the business world, managers are beginning to recognize more and more the growing demand or need of the people working for them to feel a part of the organization. Employees want to be "in the family" and have a say in the things and affairs that affect their lives.

This driving need has spawned all kinds of industries with appeals like, "you should belong to our exclusive racket club," and "everyone is learning to disco, why don't you?" and "everyone is wearing these latest styles. We have them in stock waiting for you."

Point of Application: Can the content of your message be shown to be a benefit or need satisfier for your audience in the area of *social acceptance need?* Will your message provide an opportunity for someone to get in on "the latest," "the newest," "the most popular," or will it show them a way to make friends, or help them relate to others, or teach them a new skill such as public speaking?

4. Self-Esteem Need: "I need self-respect and appreciation from others." We all have a need to feel important to ourselves and to others. That is why once we are in the herd, we want to be special to the herd. We want to be recognized as unique and not just as one of the others. This is the level of *self-esteem* that emerges after the other levels of need—*survival, security, social acceptance*—have been at least partially satisfied.

This *self-esteem need* also manifests itself in looking for responses from others in the forms of respect, recognition, attention, status, reputation, and appreciation. This is the most powerful level of personal motivation for the majority of people, this drive for personal importance and the need to be praised along the way.

Industries and businesses have learned to tap this source of drive in their employees. They have learned that a person operating on this level of human need will be strongly motivated by a word of appreciation or a public note of recognition. Even money, at this level, becomes a prime motivator as a symbol that "the boss thinks I have worth." The raise is an appeal to ego satisfaction, not simply survival need.

People operating on this level reach out for items of prestige to enhance their uniqueness. They purchase expensive cars, a beautiful home, the best, the most expensive, the most exclusive. This is the reason that you can be turned down by this man on a twenty-thousand-dollar life insurance policy, but end up selling him a two-hundred-thousand-dollar policy. He doesn't need survival money but he sure loves the prestige that goes with owning an expensive policy. It speaks to his ego and sense of self-worth.

Frustration arises on this level of need when a person is ignored, not appreciated, gets no feedback, and faces indifference. This is an attack on his ego and sense of self-worth, and raises problems in people relations. The implications for dealing with employees are obvious.

As a speaker, if you are addressing an audience of executives, you need to be prepared to "tune in" to this level of need. You need to be careful not to give the impression that you are "talking down to them" or "treating them like children." You need to respect the reality that you are in an ego arena.

You should include in your speech those positive strokes that will convey to your audience that you recognize their achievements, status and right to be appreciated. I made a simple mistake in this point in one of my speeches to a professional gathering of men. At my conclusion, the chairman thanked me and said, "We can all see that Dick Milham is a real professional in what he does, and I want him to know that we are professionals also." The next time I was invited to speak to them you can be certain I "tuned in" to their ego status.

Point of Application: Can the content of your speech be shown to be a benefit or need satisfier for your audience in the area of *self-esteem need?* Will your message stroke egos, show appreciation, make recognitions, appeal to status, offer items of prestige, or give help in personal development?

5. Self-Achievement Need: "I need to reach my full potential and do what I've always wanted to do." This level of need seems to finally come to the surface after all the other needs are satisfied to some adequate, although incomplete, degree. The person has enough money to survive. He has some security and has felt the demands of and responded to the drives of social and ego need; and now he just wants to be "his own man" and do the things "he's always wanted to do."

Sometimes a radical change in life style takes place. The person might go back to school, or leave a very lucrative position to open up a bait shop, or start a Christmas tree farm.

This person will be in the minority in your audiences, but he is to be contended with. He will not respond to the typical appeals to "be on the Presidents list" or "win a trip to Hawaii." He's been "through it all" and now he is slightly immune to those levels of personal motivation. He just wants to get on with the adventure of enjoying life as he sees it.

These people are motivated by a speaker who can be sensitive to that spirit and speak on "reaching for your dreams," "taking a chance," and "never letting yourself dry up and blow away."

I'll never forget being at a meeting of retired persons. The guest speaker was going through the typical routine of decrying that "Old people are being forced to retire at the height of their value; having to leave their jobs when they could go right on for another ten years."

An old gentleman rose to his feet right in the middle of the speaker's remarks and said, "I don't know where you are getting your information, but we love being retired. I wouldn't go back to my job if they made me president of the company. Let me tell you something; people don't die because they retire from their jobs, they die because they retire from life! Don't weep for me. We're having the best years of our lives!"

Point of Application: Can the content of your message be shown to be a benefit or need satisfier for your audience in the area of *self-achievement?* Will your message help someone reach for a long-time dream or take a chance in the adventure of life?

We have looked briefly at the catalogue of human needs. Obviously, the members of your audience are not all on the same level of need; and individual people themselves are operating on several levels at the same time. We are talking here about primary concerns in order to "tune in" to the audience; but every area of human need can be touched on in the course of your speech.

LOOKING AT HUMAN NEED AND GREED

Some matters like making money go across the board and touch on all the needs. A subject like "How To Make a Bundle" would appeal to someone on a *survival level*, "money to just stay alive," a *security level*, "a retirement income," a *social acceptance level*, "able to buy a membership in an exclusive country club," a *self-esteem level*, "able to buy an expensive beach cottage," and a *self-achievement level*, "Now I have the money to do what I really want to in life."

Another matter that is closely akin to this and also goes across the board is what psychologists have called "the desire to own worldly goods." This need to own things is a fundamental urge in our nature. This is obvious since the possession of things helps to satisfy our need at every one of the levels.

This desire to own also gives us the key to understanding the operation of the confidence man. His first objective is to appeal to greed which, according to the researchers, is one of the most stable and effective ways to influence people. They are always looking for "something for nothing."

Greed, the desire for an excessive satisfaction of some need, cannot, because of its very nature, be completely satisfied. That is why the confidence man is able to operate. He appeals to this basic desire for ownership but places it beyond the range of the reasonable to the arena of "get all you can, it's easy!"

The persuasive speaker looks to move people by appealing to their needs within the framework of what his message can honestly do for a person. The confidence man looks to "fleece the sheep" by making promises that appear to be honest, but are beyond reasonable bounds. The reason he can get away with it, is that the desire for excessive satisfaction, greed, tends to blind people to the reality that, "it's too good to be true!"

The speaker of integrity tries to work within the boundary of people's needs. The confidence man goes after people's greed!

The summary point of this whole section on human needs, that will also serve as the foundation for the rest of the chapter is simply, "The purpose of your speech, your ideas, your promises is acceptable to a person only to the extent that he feels it benefits him in some way." Nothing we can offer anyone has any value if divorced from this power principle of persuasion.

FOUR QUESTIONS YOUR AUDIENCE IS ASKING ABOUT YOUR SPEECH:

Whenever you stand in front of an audience to speak, there are usually four questions running through their minds about your message:

1. What is the purpose of your speech?
2. In what way will it benefit me?

3. Can you prove it?

4. What action are you asking me to take?

The crucial question that provides the switch to Charis-Magic power is, "In what way will it benefit me?" Many speeches answer more than adequately the other three questions, but leave this crucial one out almost completely. As an illustration, I will use a topic I suggested earlier in this book, "The Laser Beam—Stairway to the Stars."

Suppose the speaker's purpose is to get the group he is addressing to support a proposed bill to increase funding for the development of the laser beam. He states his case with some strong persuasive arguments for the need to increase the budget:

> "The laboratory is understaffed and their wages are lower than others in the same industry." (fact)
>
> "The equipment is slightly antiquated and slows down the research process." (fact)
>
> "Many of those in manufacturing need the advanced results of our research to increase their production." (fact)
>
> "Because of certain unique properties, the laser beam will provide an improved communication link with spacecrafts." (fact)

These are all good sound reasons, backing up and proving the purpose of his speech. At the conclusion, the speaker makes his final appeal. He asks that the members of the audience write their congressman and put in a strong word of support for the proposed legislation (action requested).

The speech is ended. The applause is polite. The speaker leaves, feeling he has done his job adequately; but has he? Where in his presentation did he answer the question, "How will the passing of this legislation benefit me?" For some reason he has failed to build into his content the relationship of this proposed action to the needs of the audience. He could have said such things as:

> "The laser beam can bounce off an approaching enemy plane or ship and tell us immediately its distance and speed. It can give our nation a tremendously effective

warning system against a sneak attack." (appeal to *security need*)

"Laser gyroscopes are being developed as guidance systems so accurate they can zero our bombs in on an enemy target and save us all from nuclear destruction." (appeal to *survival needs*)

"Surgeons have developed the laser to do amazing operations. They can burn away diseased tissue and even perform delicate eye surgery with the beam. With the research going on now, I wouldn't be surprised if one of you in this room will be helped or even have your life saved by the future development of the beam in surgical procedures." (appeal to *security/health* need)

"All the nations of the world are working on this laser beam. Some for its use as a powerful weapon, others for peaceful applications; but we can't allow ourselves to be second best in this race. The greatest nation in the world can't let some other country take this potential and possibly shove it down our throats one day!" (appeal to *self-esteem/prestige* need)

Now, with this material, the speaker has something to "hang his appeal on." Now, when he asks the audience to write their Congressman, they are able to see how that act will benefit them in some present or possibly future way. This is the power principle of persuasion: "Always translate your facts into some relevant benefit for your audience." When this is accomplished you can move them to respond and do whatever you want them to do.

APPLYING THE "SO WHAT?" TEST
TO YOUR SPEECH

When you finish preparing your materials for your next speech, push yourself away from the desk and ask "So What?" Ask what difference, if any, will your message make in the lives of people, and to what degree will your content reach them where they live? A criticism leveled by a leading theologian at the preaching of his day was, "The preachers are answering questions that nobody's asking!" Are you loading your content with irrelevant material that has little bearing on your case, or are you making a critical examination of it for relevancy to your arguments? The "So What?" test will help you examine your purpose, your arguments, your desired action; but most of all, it will force you to check on how well you have applied your content to the needs of your audience.

Over the years I have used this "So What?" test in the form of creative imagining. As you are preparing your material, imagine a parrot sitting on your shoulder, looking down at your paper. Whenever you finish a thought, a point, an illustration, imagine the parrot leaning into your ear and squawking, "So What?"

Through the years, this bird has forced me to keep my material relevant, has prevented me from padding my content with cute but powerless pieces and has made me get down to the business of applying my content to human need. In many practical ways this "bird on my shoulder" is more like a "monkey on my back."

During one of my consulting assignments I used this "So what?" technique to help me develop an approach to a problem posed to me by a state government official. The problem was one that was affecting almost all government transportation programs; the roads, streets and bridges were wearing out faster than they could be maintained.

There were reasons: the decreasing revenue from gasoline sales, the inflation of the dollar that limited its power, the especially damaging winters that wreaked havoc on almost all construction.

And there were proposed solutions, one of them being to increase the taxes on gasoline by one or two cents a gallon; but how would you approach an already angry public with that bit of news? How would you present the problem to them in such a way that would at least be palatable and have a chance to gain their support? This was not an easy situation since the public was already fed up with people reaching for their wallets.

There was considerable talk about getting the message to the grass roots and building a groundswell of public support. In a conference, I asked to see the proposed material that would be used in speeches prepared for civic clubs and

Chambers of Commerce and the like. The *purpose* was clear: to gain public support for an increase in gasoline taxes.

The *arguments* were clear and analytical. No one could question the logic. Charts, graphs, statistics all bore out the same conclusion: an increase was necessary to maintain the road systems. The *desired action* was also evident: support the tax increase proposal.

After considerable discussion, I asked the key question, "So What? What difference does all this mean to me where I live? All I can see is that you fellows are going to be out of a job unless I come through with my money."

I could see the look of surprise. "Now, don't take this personally. I just want you to see how this is all getting through to John Q. Public. He is saying, "I couldn't care less. What have you said to me that makes any sense to me and would motivate me to give up my money? What are you proposing that will benefit me?"

"It's obvious," one of the men snapped back. "that you are going to get better maintained roads."

"Well, that might make good sense to you, but I can't eat it the way you're serving it up. What does that mean—better roads?"

"It means," he snapped again, "that they will be safer."

"Hold it! What did you say?"

"I said they would be safer."

"Safer! . . . now we're beginning to communicate. Now that word makes sense to me. Let's see if I understand what's at stake here. Do you mean to tell me if you don't get this money, that our roads are going to be dangerous to drive on?"

"Yes, not only the roads, but the bridges also."

"Now, you're talking to me straight, right? You're not trying to pull some kind of scare tactics on me?"

"No, I can show you the charts and figures right here."

"No thanks, I've had enough of that; but what you are telling me is that I am in danger, and my child who drives my car is in danger, and my daughter driving down from upstate to see me with my little grandchild by her side is in danger!

"Now, let's see if I'm getting this. You mean to tell me that in case my home catches on fire, the fire engine might break an axle in a pothole on the way to save me, and if I have to be rushed to the hospital for emergency surgery the ambulance coming after me might be delayed by a washed-out bridge?

"Now, I think you're getting through to me. Safety—I understand that kind of language. I've said all this, maybe too dramatically, to make a simple point. If you are going to get the support of the public, you are going to have to reach them with your story on a level that will make them willing to give up their money.

"You are going to have to make them see that the alternative to your proposal is too repugnant to consider. Then you'll get their support."

I reworked the material for them, adding strong security need impact, and helped them relate the story to "where the people live." The resulting response was encouraging and supportive, coming from a public concerned about their families being out on safe roads.

The test of "So What?" can be a powerful tool in your speech preparation. Utilize it and let it open the door to increasing Charis-magic power!

PREPARING A REMINDER OF HUMAN NEEDS

Let me suggest a small aid that will be invaluable to you in reminding you of the suggestions in this chapter. Prepare a small index card as follows:

I am your *audience.* I have certain needs:

1. *Survival:* "I need to stay alive."
2. *Security:* "I need to feel safe from danger and threats."
3. *Social Acceptance:* "I need love and a sense of belonging to the group."
4. *Self-Esteem:* "I need self respect and appreciation from others."
5. *Self-Achievement:* "I need to reach for my dream."
   Say something to me that will be a *benefit* and help me satisfy one or more of these needs.

Carry the card with you next time you go to listen to a speaker and ask to what degree he met the needs of those in the audience. Put him to the "So What?" test and see if he comes up wanting in this most critical of all speaker's assignments, applying the content to the needs of the audience.

Use the card as a reminder before you speak. Remember that there are people in your audience on every level and they are looking to you to translate your message into the terms that speak to them "where they live." The end result of all this— Charis-magic power!

A BRIEF REVIEW OF THE FIRST EIGHT CHAPTERS

From the perspective of the speaker's role, Charis-magic power depends on two psychological conditions:

1. The speaker's personal expectation of power. (Chapter One)
2. His ability to build a relationship of trust (a trust zone) with his audience. (Chapter Two)

In order to build this relationship of trust, you must convince your audience that you are the kind of person who can be trusted. You do this by giving them certain assurances about the kind of person you are. (Chapter Three)

1. "You are friendly and not a threat." (Chapter Four)
2. "You know what you are talking about." (Chapter Five)
3. "You are sincere and can be believed." (Chapter Six)
4. "You care about each one personally." (Chapter Seven)
5. "You have a message that will benefit each one." (Chapter Eight)

The key to Charis-magic power is synergism, the balanced blending of these assurances to produce an effect that is greater than its parts. Each one standing alone has some effect, but when they are brought together, they produce Charis-magic power.

In the remaining chapters I will deal with some practical matters. I will share what I consider the best way to outline a speech for Charis-magic power (Chapter Nine). I will show you how to find relevant and fresh illustrations and how to test them for Charis-magic power (Chapter Ten). In Chapter Eleven, I will share certain techniques of mental preparation and deal with the actual delivery of the speech itself. Chapter Twelve will show you how to unleash the power of enthusiasm. I will conclude with a collection of material that can help you energize your presentations with Charis-Magic power (Chapter Thirteen).

 Nine

How To Structure
The
Charis-Magic Speech

In the opening chapters we looked at the psychological ingredients necessary to energize a Charis-magic speech. Now we are ready to investigate the actual structure of the speech itself. What follows in the next two chapters is not a primer on how to put a speech together. The textbooks are loaded with various methods of outlining a speech and are readily available.

What I have tried to do here, though, is to give you *one specific structure* that in my opinion most readily adapts itself to the power presentation and gets the job done. In the light of this objective, the following suggestions are offered.

BUILDING THE CHARIS-MAGIC OUTLINE

The structuring of the Charis-magic speech falls into seven logical steps, each one building on the other:

1. Write down your purpose.
2. Write down the response you want from your audience.
3. Write down your role as the speaker.
4. List the points you want to make.
5. Outline your presentation in Units.
6. Locate material for your Unit construction.
7. Prepare a closing that will lead to the desired response.

The most effective way to take advantage of the material to follow is to work through it with a proposed speech. Take out a note pad, get an idea or subject you would like to experiment with, and develop it as you go through each of the steps.

Step 1—Write Down Your Purpose: A speech without a purpose is like a ship without a rudder. You feel that you're in motion, but you sure aren't going anywhere! First and most critical to the structuring of the power speech is a clear sense of your purpose, objective, what it is you want the speech to do or tell.

The purpose will determine the kind of content you select, the role you will assume as the speaker and the action or response you will be looking for at the conclusion. For these reasons, it must be clearly and concisely stated at the very beginning.

In as few words as possible, write down your purpose. Do you want to sell a product, present an idea, inspire a sales force to higher production, show people how to quit worrying, discuss the work of the United Nations, propose a change in local government?

Be specific. Don't state your purpose in generalities. Instead of writing, "I want to motivate my employees," put down, "I want to raise production by 12% in the next six months." In place of, "I want people to enjoy better health," write, "I want to show people how to develop a program of jogging."

Write your purpose across the top of your note pad. Keep it in front of you constantly. All your selection of the content of your speech will be filtered through it. That material that will enhance, explain, expand, clarify, fortify, support your purpose will be eligible for consideration in your speech. That material that is superficial and unrelated to your purpose will die on the sidelines.

Classifying the Charis-magic Speech: The suggestion has been made that all speeches can be classified according to their purposes in three broad categories:

1. speeches whose primary purpose is to *inform.*
2. speeches whose primary purpose is to call for some *action,* and
3. speeches whose primary purpose is to *entertain.*

In the first category are found all those speeches that "want to teach us something." The main objective is just the transfer of information, much in the manner of a classroom lecture.

The second category covers that broad spectrum of speeches from political appeals to sales rallies, where the prime concern is to move the listener to some specific action. The speaker is not content to just have them "hear the word," he wants them to "do the word." *This is the heart of the Charis-magic speech.* It almost demands that it makes some moving impact on the life of the listener. By its very nature, encompassing the power to move people, it waits for its validation in the response of the audience.

The third category, the entertaining speech, is in a class by itself. It is designed for the moment and looks for immediate responses from the audience *throughout* its presentation.

These categories are, obviously, not mutually exclusive. As stated, the Charis-magic speech depends on good, informative content and can utilize the impact of humor in making its case.

Information can be delivered with the assistance of humor; and entertainment can be a vehicle for learning. What designates these categories is the *primary* thrust of the speech. **Step 2—Write Down the Response You Want From Your Audience:** What action do you want from your audience as a direct result of your speech? Do you want them to accept an idea, sign up for a course, take some specific action on a specific matter, understand the mechanics of a mercury switch, or sell two hundred pairs of shoes in the next two days?

We have just noted that the Charis-magic speech primarily calls for some definite action on the part of the audience. By definition it is "the power to move people." A speaker who comes to the podium without high expectations that the audience will respond to his speech in some positive and overt manner has already broken the first cardinal rule of Charis-magic power.

Write down your expectation, your desired response from the audience. At the conclusion of your speech, you will be looking for a closing illustration or thought to direct your audience to this desired response.

This pointing to a specific action in your speech is of vital importance. Of what value is it to have the power to create energy if that energy is not harnessed and channeled into some constructive end? Of what value is it to have the power to move people if the people are not directed to some purposeful activity?

Be specific. As in stating your purpose, be specific in stating your desired response. If your message has to do with the "general physical condition of today's executive," don't just ask them to make a commitment to better health. Ask them to call their physician within the next three days to make an appointment for a physical exam.

If you are there to help raise funds for a youth recreation program, just don't ask them to give some money. Ask them to make a pledge of at least $25 and have the cards waiting for them after the meeting.

Audiences are able to respond, if they choose, to specific requests and actions that are within the realm of their capacities. Nebulous or generalized requests are doomed to evoke no-action responses, because people cannot effectively act on a nebulous request.

Take a close look at your purpose, the objective of your speech, and translate it into a request for a specific and attainable action from your audience. This translating is part of the task of your closing illustration or thought and will be examined shortly.

Step 3—Write Down Your Role as the Speaker: How you see yourself in your speaking role will have a profound effect on the way you try to deliver your message to your audience. Do you see your primary function as someone called on to inform, inspire, entertain, convince, motivate, persuade, exhort, ad infinitum?

We categorized all speeches according to their purpose, to inform, to seek an action, and to entertain. We can also broadly categorize all speakers as either lecturers, persuaders or entertainers. Again, these are not meant to be mutually exclusive. A lecturer can make great use of humor to get his point across, and a persuader rests heavily upon the knowledge he has at hand.

But a Charis-magic speech requires a Charis-magic speaker, and by definition he must be a persuader, a person who has the power to move people. Everything he says and does should be directed at getting a response from his audience. If you come to the podium seeing yourself primarily as a teacher coming to impart wisdom or a humorist coming to be cute, you can be certain that your Charis-magic potential will be greatly weakened if not totally wiped out.

You have come to do business. You may be brilliant and you may be extremely witty, but the name of the game is power. You are called upon as a Charis-magic speaker to see yourself as the catalyst that explodes it into the present moment.

Step 4—List the Points You Want to Make: The first move in actually structuring your speech and getting your content together is what I call "creative brainstorming." With your purpose laid out clearly in front of you, let your mind fly to the winds and write down all the ideas, points, insights that come flashing into your mind.

Find what you consider to be your strongest point on the subject, write it down, and let it trigger your mind to other insights. Draw primarily from your own experiences and feelings about the subject rather than trying to find out what others have said.

At this stage in your outline's development, stay away from libraries and trying to research the subject. You will only tend to confuse yourself. Later you can use the resources to help fill out your outline, but for now go after your material by putting down your own thoughts.

If your subject isn't of enough interest to you to spark enough material for your outline, drop it. Charis-magic power doesn't come from researching someone else's convictions, but from expressing your own.

Carry a notebook around with you and, every time you find a piece of input for your outline, jot it down. Discuss the subject with someone else. You will be able to accumulate an amazing amount of material when you are able to bounce if off another person. He might drop a word, or make a comment, or pose a question that will spark your mind to new insights and thoughts.

Let your mind wander and let the ideas grow and develop momentum. You will be surprised at how swiftly the material will accumulate. Work at it in a dozen different ways, but always remember, in the final analysis what really counts is how you feel on the subject. That is what your audience wants to hear.

Step 5—Outline Your Presentation into Units: From all these ideas you have accumulated, select a few strong points that you feel are critical and important to support the purpose of your speech. The key word here is few. Your outline should be built on several points that can be built as independent Units.

The reasoning behind this kind of structure goes right back to the objective of this book. We want to get our material into a power framework. By this I mean, get it into a form that can be flexible enough to allow you to adjust it immediately for different situations, different audiences, different time allowances.

To do this, the outline and structure must be simple. That is why I say, get a few strong points. Build them into independent Units that can stand on their own, like beads in a string of pearls.

Using this approach, each Unit can be developed independently of the others; and, like the beads on the string, each Unit can be removed, added or realigned in relation to the other Units.

This structure leaves you free to be fast on your feet. Depending on the situation and the audience, you can add to or take away from the content without having the whole structure fall like a house of cards.

My first "motivation speech" evolved with the application of this Unit principle. I wanted to develop a message on the common traits of successful men. I did my brainstorming, drawing on my experiences, my observations and insights, and developed a simple and flexible outline:

Marks of the Successful Businessman

He Has A Burning *Desire* to Succeed

He *Works Hard* and is Determined to Reach His Goals

He *Overcomes Handicaps*

He *Refuses to Accept Failure* as a Final Solution

He *Cares* about Other People

Taking the key words in each point, I went on to develop subpoints and flesh them out with illustrations and experiences. Simple enough, and quite adequate for a beginner in the speaking business. Over the years, each Unit became stronger and more independent and to this day some of the material has survived in Unit form.

The Unit construction allows your speech to throb with vitality. Units can be expanded, added, improved on, deleted as obsolete, and updated for the times. This growing, living structure allows you the flexibility to plug in new pieces of material immediately to strengthen your speech; it also allows you to delete other pieces that have lost their impact or can be replaced by stronger material.

Up to this point in building the Charis-magic speech, we have simply arrived at structuring the skeletal framework, the Unit outline. Now we need to look at putting some meat on the bones.

Step 6—Locate Material for Your Unit Construction: We are ready at this point to fill out each Unit in the outline with supporting and enriching material. First, check out any factual data you might have included off the top of your head to be sure of its accuracy and relevancy. I heard a speaker go through a whole presentation talking about the "forty-eight states" to a room filled with school teachers. Certainly it was a mental lapse, but that doesn't alter the weakening effect it had on his speech.

Then, locate material to help you make your points. Some of this could be in the form of quotes, stories, newspaper articles, poetry, humor, and the like. (See Chapter Thirteen for some examples.)

There is one form of support material that is most suited for creating Charis-magic power in your speech, and that is the personal illustration. We will spend a considerable portion of the next chapter delving into its use and potential in your speech.

To make certain that the material you are gathering has the potential to give you the impact you desire, examine it all through one criterion: will adding this material to my speech help me reach my desired objective? Will it sharpen my arguments, illustrate my point, or shed light on the issue at stake?

No matter how enticing, or interesting, or humorous the material might be, if it will not advance your purpose, unload it! What you are looking for is power production and that is keyed to the relevancy of your material. This is probably one of the most difficult lessons to learn. Good material is hard to come by and once you find a "bit" you will want to take it everywhere with you.

Sometimes it works, but sometimes it doesn't and the power speaker learns not to try and force it into a mold where it doesn't fit. Save it for another occasion or another speech, but don't weaken your present case.

Try to avoid all classic clichés, poems and illustrative "bits" that have been floating around since speakers started making speeches. This is not only a problem for the beginner; sometimes you can be caught up in a "bit" that becomes a personal treasure for you. That's fine, but to many in your audience it might have the impact of a worn-out pair of shoes.

With the gathering of your support material, you will probably find sub-topics arising naturally. Each of these, just like the main Units, can be developed as an independent sub-unit, a smaller bead on the string. They will also give you the flexibility to change, delete and improve on them.

Step 7—Prepare a Closing That Will Lead the Audience to the Desired Response: The Closing of your speech is not intended to be merely a summary, but a call to some kind of action. As we noted, it may be missing from the informative or entertaining speech, but it is a necessary ingredient of the persuasive speech.

Charis-magic, the power to move people, by its very definition requires some action to validate its character. The Charis-magic speech leaves people with a determination to act or to take a particular course of action.

Prepare a closing that will help bring this *decision to act* to reality. Make it as strong or stronger than any part of your presentation. Make it well-rehearsed and well thought out and let it embody the full impact of your speech.

There are as many suggestions as speech teachers on how to bring off the Closing of your speech. Some simply instruct you to summarize your main points in a series of short, compact outbursts. This is certainly helpful and fine for a teacher closing a lecture, but not sufficient for the Charis-magic speaker.

Others suggest leaving the audience with some question ringing in their ears, "What will *you* do to stop the progress of this enemy?" Challenging enough, but of very little power, too nebulous and non-specific; or you could end with the classic "bit" of poetry that captures some light philosophy.

All well and good, but what we are talking about here is POWER! and as far as I'm concerned, that means a *direct appeal to the emotions!* This might sound blatant on my part, but the time has come to "tell it like it is." People are touched and moved when we can reach them on the level of their instincts and feelings.

The Closing of your speech should capture this power in a form that is challenging and leads to action; and the best vehicle for that kind of Closing is the personal illustration, a story that is warm and moving and delivers the full impact of your speech.

I warned you earlier about the thin line between emotionalism and the honest use of emotions and feelings in your presentations. That warning is still up, but what I am pressing for here is the valid appeal to the audience on the level of immediate impact. The purpose of this kind of illustration is not merely to stir the emotion, but to direct the emotional power of a person to bear on the subject at hand. The audience needs to *feel* the situation.

At times, as I have also cautioned, there will be members of the audience—those who have some problem getting in touch with their own feelings—who will become uneasy around this kind of approach; but you cannot allow the few to destroy the potent energy that can be unleashed by an honest and sincere use of an appeal to the emotions.

You are looking for the most effective way to apply your message to "where the people live," and that can best be done, in my opinion, by telling a story. The technique is nothing new. It is as old as the pyramids and the parables.

Look for the power Closing that can best be told in story form. The closer the story is to you personally, the more you have a "piece" of yourself in it, the stronger will be its impact on the audience. *Look for the story!* Sometimes it will be right under your nose if you will open your instincts and feelings to "smell it out."

I was scheduled to address a company on pride and loyalty and at breakfast that morning was sharing a few thoughts with some of the employees. In the exchange one of the men handed me a gem of power. That night, to a warming response, I used it to close my message:

"You know, I have to be honest with you. For the past two days I've enjoyed my time with you, but something had me stumped. So many of you have been with this company for such a long time, unusually long; and I keep wondering what is it that holds you with such loyalty. I've been thinking about what your president said this morning, that 'a man can't wander through life with no objective, no purpose,' and I have thought about what I have sensed in all of you, a feeling of family, a feeling that you are more than an employee, and you are working at more than just a job.

"I felt it this morning at breakfast when I was asking a few of the fellows how long they had been with the company, and lovable Earl, over there, told me twenty-five years! Then he showed me a watch, a watch given him in appreciation for all that service, and then he said to me.

'You know something, before I got this watch I didn't think it would mean much to me, but just look at me now.' I looked at him and he stood proud in my eyes. Then he took the watch off and handed it to me and as I touched it and held it I felt twenty-five years of a man's life vibrating through it, and I looked Earl in the eyes, and the message I got was clear: 'it's good to give your life to a job that makes you feel proud and appreciated!'

"Congratulations, you've all chosen wisely!"

Look for the power story, the story that can translate into feelings the impact you want to deliver through your message. In the next chapter you will be given some guidelines on how to locate these power stories and on how to test them for Charis-magic power.

PUTTING THE UNIT THEORY INTO PRACTICAL USE

A prominent woman in my community, a woman of much energy and talent, approached me some months ago wanting some help with a women's club meeting she was invited to address. She had some speaking experience but primarily in the area of her personal career. Now she was being asked to tackle a speech on the problem of women preparing themselves for the prospect of having to make it through life on their own.

She was having some trouble getting it all together. She had been researching the issue, ordering pamphlets from the government, buying all kinds of magazines, and all she had managed to do was get herself inundated by material. Utilizing the steps I have outlined here, we tackled her problem:

"The first thing I want you to do is forget all your reading and research. That might come in handy later, but for right now I just want to know how you feel about the subject. Do you really feel that women should be prepared in case they have to live on their own, and, does it really make any difference to you? Now, I know that might sound ridiculous to you for me to even ask the questions, but humor me and just play the game with me for a little while."

"Well, certainly, I feel very strongly about it. Every day I meet women who are trapped in their situations because they have no skills or abilities to help get them out."

"Then you feel you can get personally and sincerely involved with the subject?"

"Yes, very easily."

"Okay, let's clarify the purpose of your speech. What do you want to say through it?"

"Well, I'd like to encourage women to learn to take care of themselves in case something happens to their husband or marriage. He could suddenly die or be disabled, or the marriage could crumble apart."

"Okay, what do you want the women to do as a result of your speech? Do you just want to educate them about the problem?"

"No, more than that. I want them to do something about it, not just talk about it."

"You see yourself as being an advocate for something you believe in then, not just a teacher trying to tell them something."

"Yes, that's exactly it!

". . . and what is it you want to persuade them to do? What action do you want them to take?"

"I want them to get off their rumps, get a skill and be ready in case they are suddenly on their own!

"Okay, good! Now let's get started on outlining your message. You certainly have no problem seeing the situation, now, what do you see as possible solutions to helping the woman prepare herself?"

"Well, first of all, she needs to get a skill that she can market; either sharpen up one she used to have or get out and learn a new one. She should consider going back to school or getting some specialized training. Just anything that will put a way to make money into her grasp."

"Okay, what else comes to mind as you are thinking about the problem?"

"Well she needs to understand about money matters. What makes the financial world tick and how to budget. She also needs to know how to establish her own credit rating in case she needs to go to a bank and borrow money on her name."

"Good start, what else comes to mind?"

"Well I imagine if she's been out of circulation for a while, either raising kids or just out of the mainstream, she may need a shot in the arm as far as her confidence is concerned. Yes, she'll need some self-improvement inputs to help her feel good about herself."

"Anything else?"

"Yes, she should honestly face the fact that one day she might be living alone and she should get ready for that and prepare herself now!"

"Okay, one final question. Do you know any woman personally who has gone through this experience of suddenly finding herself on her own, and she wasn't prepared for it?"

"Yes, I know many women in that situation."

"Tell me about one of them."

She had her material. Going back over the conversation we did some additional brainstorming, and later she did some minor research to verify her facts, and then we added a title, and the speech fell into place. Here is the Opener, the Unit outline with Sub-Units, and the story Closer:

> *Purpose:* To encourage women to prepare to take care of themselves.
>
> *Desired Action:* To motivate women to get a job skill.
>
> *Role of speaker:* Persuader.

WHAT WOULD YOU DO IF IT ALL DEPENDED ON YOU?

There are thousands of displaced women in America today. Women over the age of 35 who, because of death, divorce or separation, find themselves looking for a job to help support themselves; and according to government statistics, twenty-six million of them do not have the necessary job skills to find gainful employment. Are you one of that growing number? (Opener)

1. *Develop A Skill* (Unit)
   (a) Get part-time work.
   (b) Go back to school.
   (c) Sharpen an old skill.
2. *Learn About Money Matters:* (Unit)
   (a) Take an adult education course.
   (b) Do the books at home.
   (c) Establish your own credit rating.
3. *Increase Your Self-Confidence:* (Unit)
   (a) Join a health spa.
   (b) Take up dancing.
   (c) Get involved in community activities.
4. *Learn What It's Like to Live Alone:* (Unit)
   (a) Talk to other women.
   (b) Pretend it's happened to you.
   (c) Attend a seminar.
5. *Do It Now Before the Fact:* (Closing Story)

Let me tell you about a good friend of mine—a woman who had it all. She had a fine home, a husband who loved her, a new business adventure in Florida, and then it happened; with sudden swiftness, her husband of thirty years was gone—a victim of a massive heart attack.

Now she faced the future alone. She knew she had to do something with her life. But look at her dilemma: her husband didn't leave her enough to live on and she is too young to draw Social Security. She has to go back to work.

But she's not prepared. For all those years she raised her family and took care of her home and loved it. It was beyond her comprehension that one day she would be the one to support herself. She joined that long line, those millions of women who are unprepared to take care of themselves.

Sad, certainly her situation is sad . . . but there may be an even greater tragedy brewing right here in this room. What about you! Are you wrapped in complacency? What if it happened to you?

Do something about your future right now! Learn a skill, educate yourself in financial matters, develop greater self-confidence, but do it NOW! Tomorrow is not just too late, tomorrow is fatal! (Action)

She went on to use this outline with great success. The material was flexible and natural. She was able to tighten it up to give a ten minute address or expand it to talk for an hour. In fact, she mentioned recently that she was thinking seriously of expanding the material to a three-hour seminar, all within the same basic structure.

Learn this technique of outlining and it will serve you in a masterful way. That's why I unashamedly and blatantly recommend it as the structure that most readily adapts itself to the Charis-magic speaker.

A POINT OF PERSONAL PRIVILEGE

Personally, I get very bored with outlines of generalized material that have no particular application. "Lists of things to do" have always left me a little suspicious that their author just threw in everything he could get his hands on. If your life is anything like mine, I know you have been bombarded by lists that promise you great wonders if you'd just go down the line and do everything listed.

For that reason, since we might be slightly immune to another list, I want to take a personal stand on behalf of the material in this chapter on speech preparation. What you have here is the best of my experience in this area from my professional background.

As you know, I have to live by my wits on the podium, and that requires a constant adjusting of my materials to meet the needs of the great variety of organizations I work for and with. If these suggestions had not worked for me time and time again, I would have been out of this business a long time ago.

If you're striving to be the best, and you want to continue to be invited by the finest, you can have no room for stale presentations and canned bits. You have to come on alive and fresh, and you have to do it again and again. That is why this structure is so liberating to me. It allows me to be flexible, like a boxer moving on his feet, and keeps me and my material on "the cutting edge."

I can toss out the content that's beginning to age, and plug in the new power. I can change it, mold it, turn it upside down and dance all over it, and it will still serve me. In fact, I can honestly say that I owe my continuing sense of excitement in my engagements partly to the fact that my material continues to surprise me.

All I am asking is that you give the Unit structure a chance to work for you. When you get in stride with it, exciting things will happen for you. For instance, you will discover that you will only need a few words of outline (Unit tip-offs) on an index card to get you through your whole speech.

As I have said so often, Charis-magic power depends on a Charis-magic speaker; and a Charis-magic speaker works within the framework of a structure that lets him go with the situation so exciting things can happen.

Take your pen and note pad, grab an idea, and go through the chapter again, and see if it doesn't happen for you!

 Ten

Building
Charis-Magic Power
Into Your Content

For over ten years I accumulated material, hundreds of newspaper and magazine clippings, cartoons, humorous bits, outlines, human interest stories, survey results. Like some literary pack rat, I was always clipping and filing and saying to myself, "Maybe I'll be able to use this in one of my speeches sometime."

All of this changed radically several years ago when, in the middle of one of my clip and file binges, I suddenly realized how many hours I was spending *looking* in contrast to the amount of the material I was really *using*. I set out to do some housecleaning, and for the next two days I went through file after file, reading and asking myself, "Is this the kind of material that I would really use in one of my presentations?"

Hour after hour I ruthlessly threw out piece after piece until I had finally distilled those files down to a small container about the size of a shoe box. Since then, I have reduced that box even more in searching for the kind of material that I felt had Charis-magic value. All of this is simply to point out the difficulty in finding support material that is fresh, relevant and has impact on the audience.

Helping you to discover the best source of Charis-magic material is what this chapter is all about; and, as the old song goes, "you'll find that happiness lies, right under your eyes, back in your own backyard."

The principle that I am suggesting you follow in this whole process is *gather now, apply later!*

Good illustration material is worth its weight in gold; and when you find something that fits the guidelines I will give you in this chapter, you will find not only one use for it, but many. A good illustration, like a good speech, is marked by flexibility. You can use it to go in a lot of different directions to support your speech. *Gather now, apply later!*

FINDING AND USING POWER ILLUSTRATIONS

1. Personal Experiences: "For example" is a powerful, magic phrase. It takes a point in your speech out of the realm of vague generalities and delivers it in a specific, concrete incident that is interesting and captivating to your audience. Audiences love to be told a story! Just think how you reacted when you were sitting through a dull speech and the speaker said, "Which reminds me of a story . . ."

I have no reservations in saying that the *best source of power stories is your own personal experience.* Sometimes we have a tendency to disregard our experiences, like the prophet in his own country, because we are so close to them; and because we haven't developed the nose to smell out their Charis-magic impact.

A telling of our own personal experiences carries great weight, because we have thrown the reality of our life behind

the words on our lips. We have opened ourselves to those
around us and said, "take a look for yourself. You are invited
to know me personally."

Begin with your own personal experiences. Start with an
inventory of events that are still playing around in your mind.
Sit down in a quiet moment and begin writing down all the
experiences that flood into your mind, or dictate a "stream of
consciousness" flow of events to your secretary. Don't look for
any deep meaning in them or try to understand how you might
apply them in a speech. Just let them happen.

You may at first feel that this brain jogging is a sterile
activity, but give it time. Soon events will come to mind and
one will trigger another, like dominoes falling. I spent three
hours one afternoon in this experiment: "selling cabbage as a
kid from a wagon," "fishing under the old bridge on Lake
Ivanhoe," "sneaking out of the house and playing in a hurricane," stepping on an alligator in the old swamp," "working
as a soda jerk and inventing a new drink," "selling my first
home as a real estate salesman," and so on.

I am still reaping the benefit from this power material and
I have barely scraped the surface. Every event has the potential
of power for those "who have eyes to see."

Rack your mind, get them down on paper, don't worry
about how you are going to use them. One of the developing
talents of the Charis-magic speaker is his ability to make an
illustration work for him. Take the illustration I mentioned
about "playing in a hurricane." Here is one adaptation of
using it as an illustration:

"People are always asking me if it bothers me to speak in
front of audiences. I can understand that, especially since surveys have shown it's the number one fear in the nation. Even
beats out dying and getting married. Well, no it doesn't, and
there's a reason. *Got to tell you a story!*

"When I was growing up in Florida, we used to have
some mean hurricanes. I can still remember, as a little boy
slipping outside in the middle of them with nothing on but a
tattered pair of shorts. What an experience, to stand in those
howling winds, to feel the salty spray slapping my body, to see
the tall pines bending and watch tree branches snapping like
twigs . . .

"... and there I'd be in the middle of it, and I would bellow to the winds, 'Come on hurricane! Try and beat me! Come on! See if you can whip me!'

"I fought the hurricane. I threw my puny weight and small frame against that titanic force *and I whipped it*. I remember how I'd feel when I'd sneak back in the house, soaking wet, my body tingling from the impact of the wind and spray. I remember how I'd bask in the glow of the knowledge that I had whipped a hurricane!

"Do you think anything bothers me now? When I stand up in front of an audience, what do I have to be afraid of? I've whipped hurricanes and nothing is tougher than that!"

From this story I would go on to a discussion of our self-image and how it affects our ability to relate to people and perform in life situations.

Originally I had no plans for this story to be used like this; but in the development of my self-image seminar I suddenly found a need for an illustration and when I looked around, there it was, tucked away quietly in my collection of personal experiences just waiting to give my material a Charis-magic boost.

A Dilemma In Pittsburgh: Again, the key is *gather now, apply later.* Another example is a simple incident that happened to me in a Real Estate meeting in Pittsburgh. I have used this story innumerable times since to illustrate the need for salespersons to stick with it and work through their disappointments:

"Some jobs are loaded with frustrations, situations you can't control and contracts that seem to fall apart at the last minute. If you're not careful you can get the "failures" out of perspective and lose a great deal of your time and energy worrying about the ones that got away. *Got a story to tell you:*

"I was in Pittsburgh a few months ago to speak at the annual meeting of one of the largest real estate firms in the area; and just before I got up, the boss came to the front of the room and called out the names of ten salespersons and asked them to come forward.

"They lined up, right across the front of the room and he said, 'Look at them . . . the biggest failures in this company!' I couldn't believe my ears. 'Look at them, lost more contracts, lost more money, lost more deals than any of you!' Now, I was supposed to follow this with some words of uplift and appreciation, and here the boss was whipping them up one side and down the other. They just stood there and took it.

"Again he said, 'Look at the failures' and he started to walk off; but then he turned, smiled and said, 'Oh, by the way, did I also mention, these also happen to be the ones who made more money, and closed more contracts and put more deals together than any of you?'

"The successful salesperson learns how to handle disappointments. In this business, when you have a stack of successes on one hand, you'll have a stack of misses on the other because you don't make them all!"

Sharing A Deeply Personal Experience: Sometimes the material is deeply personal, and for that reason the impact is powerful. These are not easy moments to share and leave you feeling completely exposed as a person, but sometimes the risk is worth the telling. On certain occasions, when the speech warrants it and the audience is "able to handle it," I share an experience that relates to "never allowing your life to dry up:"

"Because I feel that you are the kind of people who can appreciate what I am about to say, I want to share something very personal with you. I've learned a lot about living from my parents, but the most moving lesson they ever taught me caught me out in left field unexpectedly.

"While away at college, I got word that my mother had suffered a very severe heart attack. I rushed home to Florida and to the hospital to find her stretched out in very weakened condition. The doctors said that she would make it, but in the days ahead she would have to radically change her life style.

She was a woman of tremendous energy and vitality, and telling her to slow down, get long hours of sleep, and take her medication faithfully, were almost wasted efforts. She knew only one way to enjoy life and that was flat out. Her body just couldn't seem to keep up with her boundless energy.

"Again, she suffered another severe heart attack and this time I decided I was going to tell my mother how to live. Me . . . I was going to tell *her* how to live, a woman who crossed the ocean in a boat as a teenager to a land of unknown tomorrows, a woman who had more life in her little finger than I had in my whole body, a woman who lived through the depression by the sweat of her hands and brought us up by the seat of our pants ... I was going to tell her how to live.

"I went into the hospital room and was taken aback by the sight of the needles in her arms and the tubes in her nose, but I had to have my say.

"Mama, we all love you so very much; and the doctors say you can be with us a long time if you'd only take care of yourself and get your sleep and take your medicine."

"I'll never forget the moment; she looked me in the eyes and her hand reached over and touched mine, and in the ancient language of our people she said, 'My love, my very eyes, let your mama die... *alive!*"

"A few years later ... she did; and we celebrated her dying, a testament to life! Now, I don't recommend her style to you. I don't suggest that you run out and disregard your doctor's orders, but I do recommend her spirit with everything in me! We live in deeds, not heartbeats, in breathing deeply of the moment, not in years. Some live more of life in a few years than those whose blood creeps through their veins. Die *alive!*"

Many times, sharing a story like this will lead you to another story. Rarely have I ever told about this moment in my life without someone coming up to me afterwards with some equally moving experience. On one particular occasion, I had spoken at a meeting where a man was honored for his work on behalf of his Association. He was a striking man, tall, silver haired, warm, and with a touch of elegance. I had just finished listening to some "flyweight mentality" who was trying to tell me how to do my business, when he approached.

"I just wanted to thank you for sharing that story about your mother with us tonight. No one here knows, but I have only a few months left to live, and I too have decided to *die alive.* I will carry that thought with me to my death."

Every one of us is a potential gold mine of personal experiences. This is the kind of stuff that power is made of, the more personal, the more powerful; the closer to realities, the greater the impact. Find the experiences, collect them for the moments that you will need them and let them work for you in building Charis-magic power.

2. Stories Told To You By Others: Another productive source of finding power illustrations is the experiences of others. Get into the habit of picking people's minds. Just consider all the thousands of stories that are floating around you in the experiences of your friends and even complete strangers. They are like gold mines waiting for you to work. The prospects are incalculable and every one of them can be personalized by an introductory phrase:

"While we were having lunch . . .," "Just as we approached the twelfth hole . . ,"

Learning From An Old Pro: "He got on the plane in Atlanta and took the seat beside me . . . and I noticed a ring on his right hand. I just had to ask about it, especially when I got a glimpse of the word "Pro" on it. He was a gentle giant kind of a man; friendly and vibrating with warmth. But back to the ring.

He took it off and handed it to me and said, "Professional Football Hall of Fame . . . quarterback; but so many years ago you probably wouldn't remember."

I liked him. He was easy to talk to and just filled with all kinds of great stories. I found out as the flight continued that he was now a scout for a national football team; and I asked him about player injuries and how it affected the game.

"There's no way you're going to play this game without taking some cracks. One of the things we look for in a man is whether he can play hurt, whether he is tough enough to take the pain and come back again for more!"

There are always obstacles to be overcome; that's the nature of life. You will always find reasons for not getting into the game, logical and reasonable answers; but the mark of the great ones is their ability to "play hurt, play tough," play when every jar sends shock waves of pain through their body. That's the name of the game of life; and those who learn not to buckle under at the first sign of pressure are those who are the victors."

Everyone has a story to tell, a stick of dynamite that you

can add to your power material. The secret is in learning to listen and being "tuned in" to the potential of what you hear. During one of my seminars for an insurance company in Chicago, I heard a story that helped me illustrate a point I was trying to drive home in some of my presentations.

Racing For Second Place: "I can understand why a person who has been a failure all his life has such a hard time reaching for success. He has no experiences of winning to relate to. All he knows is how to be a loser. What I don't understand, though, and what to me is the great mystery of motivation, is not why unsuccessful people are not successful, but why successful people limit their success. They say "I am good for just so much success, but no more."

Part of the problem has to be in the way we see ourselves, in our own self-images and in the patterns we learned since we were children. *Got a story to tell you:*

"During one of my recent seminars, we were delving into the reasons that we don't stretch for success, and one young insurance salesman stood up and shared a story with us. He said, 'When I was a young boy I used to race bicycles. All the kids in the neighborhood would come over and every afternoon I'd race them and beat them.

"Day after day it went on, until one day I got tired of it. Every time I'd win, back they'd come. One afternoon I was flying along and this one kid was right on my tail and I thought to myself, 'You know, if I let that kid pass me and he comes in first, then tomorrow they will all go over to his house and leave me alone.' So I slowed down, and he passed me, and I came in second . . . and do you know, the next day they all went over to his house. I learned something that day. I learned how comfortable it is to be in second place with no hassles.'

"Let me ask you something, okay? When you find yourself leading this company in sales, have you ever slowed down and let someone else pass you?" He slowly smiled and looked back at his boss, in the corner of the room.

"Well, if you want to know the truth, yes I have!"

"How come?"

"Well, if I do it this month,' then he pointed to his boss, "he'll be on my back to do it again next month!"

He had learned! It's comfortable to be in second place: to

stay out of the limelight and just nibble at the corners of success. He was a successful salesman who had limited his success."

The stories available are boundless; they are all around you. With that wealth of material, it seems almost a crime to be filling your speeches with clichés and worn-out words. Pick the minds of those around you, and you will discover gems of power.

3. Gathering Stories From Other Sources:

Always be on the lookout for material. Whenever you are reading a magazine or newspaper, keep this thought in front of you: "Would this item be something I can use to give my speech Charis-magic power?" After a while it will be almost like second nature to smell out the power illustrations.

Over the years, my wife has learned the kind of material that appeals to me, and she is always cutting out articles and the like for me to check through when I get home. In just a few minutes I am able to scan through them, keep the ones I feel have some potential and toss the rest away. Find someone who might enjoy helping you like this. You'll be amazed at how quickly your support material will grow.

The majority of my gathered material comes from the daily newspaper; those little gems of interest of the "man bites dog" genre. I am constantly discovering unusual and potent bits that help make my material come alive.

When trying to help young people see their uniqueness and reinforce their sense of self-worth, I often share this story:

16 Million Years and Running: "You are special! In a vast universe that transcends our understanding you are unique and special! There's no one like you in this spectacular array of space and time. You want to know how big it all is and how special you are? Well, *I have a story to tell you:*

"A few years ago some Dutch astronomers put their telescopes into outer space and they found a chunk of universe so big it makes my skin crawl. I'm not sure how to tell you how big, but let me try.

"Suppose one of you could be rocketed up to this object in space, and we put a pair of good, tough sneakers on you and started you running across the diameter of that vast object . . . at the speed of light!

"Now, according to my last calculation, that means you'd be moving at 186,282 miles every second ... that means every time I snap my finger you would have covered 186,282 miles; that's seven times around this earth ... every second! Now that's moving.

"At that speed you would be able to go across the diameter of that object in space in just a little over 16 million years! Now that's long. Longer than my car payments.

"... and there you are, in the middle of that kind of awesome universe and you are alive and breathing. Think of it, out of all the billions of possibilities of life, you are alive; and out of all the conceptions that did not take place, you are alive! You have already beat astronomical odds ... you are breathing and alive; and you should walk tall, love being who you are, and not let the users of life wipe their feet all over your body, and your mind, and your spirit!"

Gather, then apply. This has been the operating principle of this chapter. Find the unusual and eventually you will find a place for it to flex its potent impact. Here is a story that I gathered two years before it ever became a living illustration in one of my speeches. The setting is a seminar on self-image building and the point being made was the effect of poor inputs into our image:

"In our self-image we have all kinds of expereinces from early childhood to the present moment. Many of these experiences are destructive in nature. We need to expose them and rid ourselves of them. *I've got a story to tell you:*

Diamonds In The Freezer: "A farmer in Wisconsin was out in the middle of a hot and humid summer day plowing his fields and he came across an unusual sight. In the center of his field he discovered an icy, blue glacier-like mass melting in the sun. He knew it had to come from the sky somewhere since it wasn't there the last time he came through.

"He called the university and they sent a man from their geology department to inspect it, but he had little success. They called the state capitol for assistance and a man was on his way. The farmer wanted to preserve the treasure, so he took all the food out of his freezer and chopped off huge chunks of the blue glacier and loaded them into his freezer for safekeeping.

"When the expert arrived, he didn't take long clearing up the mystery. It seems that a commercial jet was flying over that farm at about fifty thousand feet that day, and for some unknown reason the pilot decided to eject the holding tanks for the restrooms, and as that liquid mass came through the freezing altitude, it was formed into the icy, blue glacier that the farmer discovered in his field.

"He thought he had diamonds in his freezer, when in truth he had . . . well, you figure it out.

"What have you got in your freezer? What kind of destructive and wasted experiences have you stored in the caverns of your mind? It's time to expose them to the light and let them melt away and free you to enjoy a fuller life."

Always be alert to the power illustration. Learn to identify its attributes and store it away for some future opportunity to apply it with Charis-magic power. In the section to follow I will give you some guidelines to help you determine which illustrations have the power potential.

TESTING THE ILLUSTRATION FOR POWER

In my estimation, there are four tests that a piece of illustrative material should pass before it is considered for your speech: is the illustration *rare, relevant, personal* and *easily applied*? Again, the point in passing this test is to make it eligible for using. Remember, *first gather, then apply*.

Rare, The First Test: The material should be unusual, not the run of the mill occurrence that has lost any impact. Stories of the "man bites dog" variety, or with an O'Henry twist, or some unusual facet, like the woman who had her husband buried off the 18th green of the local golf course—"He loved it so much, and spent so much time on it, I know he'll be happy." The club members didn't mind; in fact, one was quoted as saying, "Hey, that's great with me. If I overshoot that green, maybe a friendly hand will come up out of the ground and tap it back on for me."

. . . or the surprise when a 13 year old boy in North Carolina was found to have a tooth growing in his foot, a rare case of "genetic misdirection" his doctor said. His dad's comment was, "No wonder I couldn't keep him in shoes, he kept eating them up."

. . . or the bizarre story about a man who took a passage in the Bible literally and cut off a foot, and a hand and gouged out an eye with a pocket knife. The attending physician commented, "I am amazed that he could tolerate such self-inflicted pain, and puzzled how he could get through the bones with just a pocket knife."

Look for the quality of rare and unusual. Don't try to make sense of it or apply it; just store it away and its time will come. For example, here's a story that I finally used to make a point about having "credibility." In Florida, a man went on trial for attempted murder. He threw his wife in a large pit and then tried to cover her over with dirt using a huge bulldozer. At his trial his defense was, "it was an accident!"

Relevant, the Second Test: There's an old saying, "nothing's as old as yesterday's newspaper. Constantly quoting the distant past will rob you of much vitality in your speeches. You can't keep coming up with museum pieces and expect the public to feel that they are in a twentieth century atmosphere. Many people equate "old" with "old-fashioned." That's a shame, but you must recognize that fact.

Use very few references to events in the distant past. Not that I don't have a great admiration and love for the past; but *speaking is a now event,* a present moment, and it has a right to be filled with a sense of freshness like today's headlines. Vitality flows from this kind of "vibe" in a presentation.

"One hour of prime time television can cost the advertiser as much as $400,000 an episode with one minute going for as high as $230,000; and we call it 'free' T.V."

Even in the arena of telling about your personal experiences, don't dwell in the past. Plug in some now, contemporary experiences to give the flavor of action in the present. If you stay in the past, audiences can't help but wonder, "but what's he done lately?"

Some of my most powerful moments in opening a meeting have come when I've held up a newspaper hot off the press to point out a story, or quoted from a magazine I "picked up at the airport newsstand on the way over here." Feel the flush of vitality whenever you tap the present moment.

Personal, the *Third Test:* Does the illustration deal with some facet of human nature that people can easily identify with? Here is the great storehouse of quotes that come from the human spirit.

For example, the words of last year's Nobel prize winner Arno A. Penzias on the eve of receiving his award for his work in "cosmic microwave background radiation. The prize came on the 40th anniversary of his family's deportation from Nazi Germany as Jewish refugees,

"I guess it's no longer fashionable to believe in the American dream, but I am really a beneficiary of that . . . to come with nothing but to be able to achieve something."

. . . or the moving story of Dr. Christiaan Barnard, the great surgeon of heart transplants, holding out his own hands and speaking about the arthritis ravaging through them, about the physical pain he was tolerating, about how he has lost his tremendous drive, and how he still weeps at the death of one of his patients.

. . . or the simple words of Leopold Stokowski, the legendary conductor, in a television interview, "no emotion . . . death!"

. . . or the happy face of Ernie Banks, the Chicago Cubs great, as he addressed a group of businesswomen and reminded them, "I always tell myself, someone out there has my money in their pocket."

The words don't have to fall on the lips of the great or legendary. Life is filled with the "little people" who have touched us with their acts of loving and desperation.

For example, there was a young man who was desperate to win back the love of his girlfriend, so he started out early one morning and crawled on his hands and knees over sixteen miles to her house. When he arrived there, his knees and hands were bloody and he was near exhaustion from his six-hour ordeal. Her comment, "It was a dumb thing to do!"

Easily Applied, the *Fourth Test:* Does the illustration or story have a simple, uncomplicated plot? Sometimes stories are so involved that by the time you lay out all the detail, the "thrill is gone." Mark this well; if your story takes more than a few lines to set up, drop it! Your story should be easy to tell, simple to understand and end with a punch or twist that gives it power.

Like the 78-year-old woman who kept the mummified body of her husband, who had been dead for three or four years, with her. When they discovered him (along with $7,000 in uncashed V.A. checks), and asked her why she kept him, she said, "I just didn't have the heart to give him up."

This story applies itself almost immediately to a dozen different situations: "people who can't give up old habits," "businesses that still do things the way they've always done them and refuse to change," "those who cling to old ideas, or discarded methods." The applications can go on and on with the tag line, "and if you ask why they keep doing things the way they are doing them, or why they still hold the same old ideas, if they were really honest they probably would say, "I just don't have the heart to give them up."

... and there's the story about a crippled man who pushed himself in his wheelchair eight miles to a hospital with his sick fourteen-year-old son on his lap because he didn't have money for a bus or cab. "When you want to do something," he said, "you just don't say it, you do it!" The applications are obvious.

... or the words of Bill Jordan, the winner of Missouri's Cow Chip Throwing Contest with a 174 foot toss. When he was asked to give some advice to the youngsters, he said, "Wear gloves." I'm not sure how I'll end up applying this one, but I can hardly wait to see.

... or take the case of Barbara Smith of Washington who took a baseball bat to her 1964 Oldsmobile after it failed to stop once too often. When the police arrived, they found one battered car, a broken baseball bat, and a contented 29-year-old woman. "I feel good," she said, "that car's been giving me misery for years, and I killed it."

Look for the simple endings, straightforward and uncomplicated. They are easiest to fill with Charis-magic power.

Test your illustrations. Are they rare, containing some

unusual or surprising twist? Are they relevant, throbbing with the sense of a "now" involvement with life? Are they personal, filled with all the magnificent diversity of the human spirit? Are they easily applicable, lending themselves to a simple and powerful conclusion?

Not every story can contain all these elements in equal parts, but you will discover that your most powerfully moving or effective material will be marked by these attributes.

HOW TO USE HUMOR EFFECTIVELY

One of my favorite cartoons shows an audience sitting somber-faced and somewhat bewildered, looking up at the podium where there is a speaker doubled over in laughter, tears running down his cheeks, slapping one knee with his hand; and the caption reads: "Well, enough of this humor."

I have seen grown men die and nearly cry because of their ineffectiveness to handle humor. Nothing will kill you quicker than coming out with a rash of stale bromides or "blowing a punch line," that wasn't funny anyway.

Humor, to be "power humor" must qualify just like every other piece of material in your speech. It has no right to appear on its own merit. Unless the humor you use advances, enhances, or supports the major thrust of your message, drop it!

You get into trouble when you start telling funny stories just for the telling. My earliest attempts were disastrous. I was told that the good speakers used a lot of humor, so I tried to put together some routines like those of a stand-up comic, and they failed miserably. I soon discovered what the persuasive speaker has always known, that humor must serve as a means to an end, not be an end in itself. Humor must always justify its existence like every other piece of material in your speech by making a point, strengthening an argument or driving home a truth.

Take a close look at the humorous elements in your speeches. Do you tell them just for the telling, or are they actively supporting the thrust of your message and helping to generate Charis-magic power? Are they vital to the direction of your material or would your speech be better off without them for all the good they are doing? Be ruthless in your examination and clean house if you need to.

Finding the Humorous Story: The best source of humor, like the best source of illustrations, is found in your *own personal experiences.* The stories you tell about yourself, your family, the people you meet, are all the kind of stuff that laughs are made of.

Sharing personal stories lets you be yourself and saves you from having to assume some unnatural, comedian's role; and people love it! Audiences easily identify with humor that rises naturally out of everyday situations. Everyone knows what it is like to run out of gas "in the center lane of the freeway during the rush hour," and forget to pay a bill, "and there we were with my boss and his wife serving up a fancy dinner, and the lights went out!"

Many of your audience can identify with having a teen-ager around the house:

". . . as for me, I get no respect! Do you know what it's like to have a fifteen-year-old daughter around the house? You know the age, when they're embarrassed to have you as a father.

I came home the other day after a long, hard week on the road and walked in the front door; and the first thing she said to me was, "Dad, would you mind staying in your room tonight? I've got friends coming over and I don't want them to meet you."

. . . and I said, "but honey, they'll love me! Kids all over America just love me and think I'm great!"

. . . and she says, "Yeh, Dad, I know all about that, but you're home now . . ."

The greatest source of humor is those personal bits of living that everyone can identify with, those unusual little twists and crazy everyday kinds of things that happen:

. . ."My wife is from Wilmington, North Carolina; she talks funny. She taught this old boy from Brooklyn to eat grits and red-eyed gravy and parts of a pig I never knew existed!"

. . ."I've finally decided! I'm going to hire an archaeology team and we are going into my daughter's room and find her bed!"

. . ."Do you know what it's like to live in a house with a dog who won't let you get into your bed at night?"

Make your humor a part of the "natural" you. Let it flow as genuinely as if you were in conversation with someone. Just share those "bits and pieces" of yourself as a person "who sometimes does some really dumb things." The audience will love you for it.

Telling the Humorous Story: Without getting into a long discourse on why "some can tell 'em and some can't," let me just share a few suggestions that might improve your handling of humor:

- Let your humor be an extension of yourself as a person. Let it flow out of the richness of your personal experiences.
- Don't laugh at your own jokes. That old saying about "laugh and the world laughs with you" isn't necessarily so. You may discover that you are doing a solo.
- Don't try to explain a joke if it falls flat. If it needs explaining, you should never have told it in the first place. Remember, a story should be easily applied.
- If you want a little "bomb" insurance, put the story in someone else's mouth. Say that you "heard a speaker . . ." or "last Sunday your Minister . . ." If it falls flat you can always blame it on someone else; "it was their story, not mine."
- Stay away from offensive or sensitive humor. If in doubt, don't use it. Many a speaker has torpedoed his effectiveness and credibility by resorting to low blows. You can only hurt yourself.
- Remember that the most effective humor is what lies right at your own back door. Tap the rich resources of your experiences as a human being. The audience will love you for it.
- Test every piece of humor for Charis-magic power in your speech. Like all "support material" it must point the audience to the purpose.
- Don't forget to use humor. We all need to feel its uplifting power. If nothing else, it gives the audience a chance to "get together" on something. Laughter, you know, is a community activity.

Closing In On the Moment: You have been psychologically

prepared to expect Charis-magic power. Your purpose is clear before you and your speech has been structured into Units of power.

You have tested and selected "support material" to drive home your message and enhance your presentation, and now, the time is at hand—the time when all the pages of this book coalesce into one "moment of truth;" the actual presentation of the Charis-magic speech!

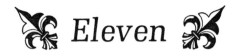 Eleven

How To
Meet and Speak
To Your Audience
With
Charis-Magic Impact

A friend of mine, who had been doing public speaking for over six years, said to me with a straight face, "I don't mind talking. I can handle that, It's having all those people out in front listening to me that gets to me." The time has come to take the suggestions of these pages and use them in the actual speaking engagement.

Over the years I have discovered that there are *four ele-*

ments that need to be considered in preparing and delivering the Charis-magic speech:

1. Your Preparation, the Key to Self-Confidence.
2. The Physical Situation, the On-Site Inspection.
3. The Audience Expectation, Finding Their Pulse.
4. The Actual Presentation, Charis-magic Power in Motion.

These four elements, as diverse as they might seem, all have an important bearing on your ability to get your speech through to your audience with Charis-magic power. The purpose of this chapter is to help you confront each of the areas so you come away feeling you have them under control.

YOUR PREPARATION, THE KEY TO SELF-CONFIDENCE

Self-confidence has always been regarded as an essential ingredient for successful speaking. This is more than the "expectation of power" we discussed in the first chapter. Self-confidence has to do with the relationship of the speaker to himself, his own self-image.

He might be able to generate the sense of "I am expecting great things!" but at the same time be saying, "but in spite of me, not because of me." Self-confidence puts the monkey right back on the speaker's back and asks, "What are you expecting from you?"

In past years I spent a lot of energy pursuing this elusive butterfly of self-confidence. All the power personalities of speechmaking told me I had to have it and without it I wouldn't get very far in my career; but none of them were too helpful in telling me *what* it is or how I could acquire it.

If you should ask me today, though, I would define this phenomenon of self-confidence as *"an inner assurance that you can get the job done!"* Isn't this what you mean when you call a person confident? Aren't you really saying "he can do what he says he can?" Isn't this what you mean when you say you have confidence in a person? You believe he can produce the promised results.

If you are a self-confident speaker, then you enter the podium with an inner assurance that you can get the job done. Obviously, this condition of mind does not spring up overnight. Whatever else might have been said about Charis-magic as a speaking event, we had better not forget that it's hard work, involving a lot of behind-the-scenes preparation. When it appears effortless to an audience, you can be assured that much sweat has been poured out to give that impression.

The Secret Of Becoming A Self-Confident Speaker: The development of your self-confidence, your inner assurance that you can get the job done when you go before that audience, is really no great mystery. Like everything else in this book, it is based on known psychological principles.

Rather than becoming involved in some long discussion at this point, let me simply share my own formula on how you can continue to grow in self-confidence. In my experiences, self-confidence comes as the result of "knowing that you know" and "practicing what you know."

Knowing That You Know: A noted psychologist observed that "the root of all fear is a lack of familiarity." This reason alone helps to explain why so many thousands of people have such a fear of public speaking. For them, speaking is a new and unfamiliar experience like parachuting out of a plane for the first time.

As an experienced speaker, though, you can also find yourself in the quandary of lacking self-confidence; and this usually results when you allow yourself to be put in the position of speaking on a subject that you are not comfortable with or you are unsure of.

Mark this well; when you are unsure of your content, you are in trouble. You will be facing your audience with your guns half-loaded, and if you run out of bullets you have no place to hide. You see, speaking allows you the unique opportunity to fail while everybody's watching. This fear of failing, of making a fool out of yourself, indicates a lack of self-confidence and needs to be attacked at the root of the problem, your subject matter.

If you feel unsure about what you are talking about, you can be certain you will experience a lack of self-confidence.

Nowhere have I ever found a substitute for solid preparation and knowledge!

The more you know about a subject, the greater your sense of self-confidence, and that's a fact! Underline this ten times: "confidence comes from knowing what you are talking about." Earlier in this book we looked at knowledge as a fundamental necessity in helping to build your trust relationship with the audience; and here we discover that knowledge is also critical to your sense of self-confidence.

Not only are you called on to impress the audience that you know what you are talking about, but here you discover that you had better know what you are talking about if you are to impress the audience.

This is one of the reasons I have insisted throughout this book that knowledge is indispensable to experiencing Charis-magic power. Don't allow yourself to be shoved out of the area of your expertise and saddled with some subject that you have no knowledge of or interest in. One of the basic rules I handed you in preparing a speech outline was to do it off the "top of your head," and if you don't have enough material, then drop the subject!

As much as I pride myself on my expertise in a variety of subjects, I find there are times when I have to say to someone extending an invitation for me to speak, "I'm really not your man. I could do a possibly adequate job on that subject, but you really want someone who is a professional in that area. Thank you for your consideration, and I look forward to helping you when my services are needed in the areas of my strength."

I had just concluded speaking at a meeting of the Wisconsin Credit Union League and was enjoying some warm moments with several new friends. In the conversation about being a public speaker, one of them commented,

"You know what bothers me? Take a man, for instance, who is a corporate lawyer and he is invited to speak at a meeting on the subject of, oh, let's say the American economy. You can just bet that about three minutes into his speech, he's going to be talking about corporate law. Now, he might start out sounding like he's going to handle the announced subject, but you just give him a little opening . . . and that's it! Now tell me, how come?"

"Because," I responded, "when you get a little nervous as a speaker or find yourself dealing with a subject you are a little unsure of, you will have a tendency to go for the area of your strength where you feel confident.

"In this case, the lawyer feels comfortable when he is talking about corporate law. He understands corporate law. He feels at home with corporate law. He feels secure with corporate law; but most of all he feels confident about his knowledge of corporate law. What he should have done was just refuse the invitation and others like it until he felt good about his knowledge of the American economy."

Self-confidence comes from knowing that you know, and the pursuit of knowledge is a powerful aide in helping this confidence grow and develop.

In a brief review let me remind you about the *basic features* you need to know about the Charis-magic speech. You need to know *your subject*, your *purpose*, your *role* as the speaker, your *desired response* from the audience. As far as your speech is concerned, you need to know that it has a strong *Unit structured outline*, that the *support materials* are personal and relevant, that the *Closing* has impact and will point the audience to a *benefit* as the result of an *action*.

You need to know, finally, that you have strewn "bits and pieces" of yourself as *friendly, knowledgeable, sincere* and *caring* throughout the content in order to build trust with your audience.

If you sense and feel confident about all these areas before your presentation you are on your way to a Charis-magic windup in your speech.

Practicing What You Know: Self-confidence also comes as a result of feeling secure in your *presentation* of the speech. This security comes as a result of practice before the speech and repeated speaking experiences. Any skill, regardless of what it is, requires repeated acts of accomplishment before any level of proficiency is reached.

Speaking in public is a *skill* that will continue to improve with repeated use. The one significant mark of the Charis-magic speaker's skill is his *flexibility*. For this reason, you should have as a prime goal the presentation of your speeches with a minimum of notes. Detailed notes tend to lock the speaker in to a single track. A word outline built on a Unit structure will leave you free to move in any direction.

No matter where you find yourself in your use of notes, *begin a systematic reduction of them*. If you have a complete manuscript in front of you, begin by taking out a bit at a time. There's certain to be some section, some illustration, some story that you can handle without reading it. Take that piece and practice it over and over, not memorizing but simply getting used to telling it; and the next time you speak, pull that section out of your manuscript and key it with a single word as a reminder.

When you feel secure in handling that bit from the top of your head, move on to another. Every time you release a piece from the page, you will enrich your presentation and build your confidence. Set as your final goal, the offering of a speech with only an index card for all your notes. When you are freed from the page, you are flexible; and when you are flexible, Charis-magic power can flow.

How To Handle Fear: How can you appear confident before an audience when your stomach is filled with stampeding elephants, your throat feels as if it's been paved with asphalt, and your eyebrow keeps twitching?

Most advice-givers will tell you to "fake it till you make it." They argue that you will be ineffective with your audience if they find out how nervous you are.

Well, that might be good advice to give a professional speaker; obviously, it doesn't make sense to put out a bundle for him and have him come to your meeting and spend the first ten minutes muttering something about how nervous he is. He gets paid to be the best, to appear before the audience with a sense of power and control over his words and actions. That's his business.

Remember, though, you are not usually considered a professional speaker in the sense of making your living at it. You are viewed as a person who is primarily in some business or profession who happens to be speaking; and for you, admitting your feelings can be a great source of persuasive power.

For the most part, your audience is not expecting you to appear as a professional speaker. In their eyes you are one of them—an ordinary person being called on to speak; and they can easily identify with your feeling of butterflies in your stomach. You have in this a source of persuasive power that the professional speaker has been stripped of.

Admitting that you are a little nervous makes you a "real" person, someone they can feel a common experience with. In our look at the assurance of *friendly* and *non-threatening*, we mentioned wrapping your power in a friendly framework. Here is an excellent example of backing off on your power by sharing your feelings, letting yourself be seen as human.

Honesty at this point will also build credibility in your words. You show the importance of your message by showing that, although you are nervous, what you have to say is more important than your fear of speaking. In their minds you are paying a personal price for getting your message across, and usually they will cheer you on.

I saw a startling example of this phenomenon of audience support for someone on the platform in an unusual setting. Each summer, for several years, I worked with the YMCA in a Values Clarification Conference for young people. Several hundred of us from the inner city of Pittsburgh to the rolling hills of Maryland would gather at Gettysburg College in Pennsylvania for a week of hammering away at coming to grips with our life values.

One of the highlights of the week was a talent show featuring any talent the young people could dig up. Some were really exceptional, others questionable, but all got a shot at the stage. Toward the close of the evening, two young girls were introduced and came to the platform, one with a guitar and the other with a flute.

They started to play and a few measures into the music the girl on the flute missed a few notes. They stopped and tried again and this time she missed a few more and then even more until finally, in frustration, she quit and tears came to her eyes.

The room was deadly silent except for her quiet sobs, and then one of the young people in the audience stood up and yelled, "You can do it!" And then another voice and another,

"You can do it! Go on; we're with you. Try it again!" Suddenly loud applause reverberated through the room and then respectful silence. The girls started again and this time they made it.

I've reflected on that experience many times and concluded that it is a powerful example of audience rapport, of one person saying to another, "I know what you are feeling. I know what it must take to be up there. You've got my support." That's why there is so much power in saying honestly, "I know you'll understand if I tell you I feel a little nervous right now."

Using this approach, I was able to help a friend make a rare public appearance. He was called to introduce a man seeking the governor's office at a fund-raising dinner. That sounds simple enough but, as likeable as Bill was, nothing short of a miracle could turn him into a polished speaker in two weeks, muttering was his forte.

The key would be to work within the scope of his natural fear and capitalize on helping him appear just as natural as he is. I met with him to help put the introduction together.

"Bill, do you really believe he's the man for the job? Do you really feel good about supporting him?"

"Yes sir, Dick. I've known him a lot of years. I guess that's why they want me to do the introducing."

Using a lot of the persuasive material found in this book, I worked to help him put together a few words that would get the job done and get the audience on his side. The night of the banquet I saw a warm, natural human being communicate with an audience with simplicity and power:

"Now, those of you who know me, know that I've got to be the worst speaker in the world (*credibility, telling it like it is*). I know that. You don't have to tell me. I'm the only man I've ever met who could fall asleep during one of his own speeches (*nice guy, poke a little fun at himself*); and I don't mind telling you, I'm nervous (*building empathy, using the fear to establish rapport*), but I'm here!

"... and the reason I'm here is because I think this is one of the highest honors I've ever had given me (*the subject is greater than the fear*).

"Let me tell you something! I've run in some high cotton in my day, and I've met all kinds of people, high and low, *(establishing his right to speak)* but I've never met a man I respected more than our guest tonight. He was born in a little farm community . . .*(introduced the body of the biographical material . . .)* . . .

". . . now, I want you to meet him. The next governor of our state, but best of all, my friend *(you can trust him),* . . ."

Use your fear for power persuasion. Use your nervousness to draw the audience to you as a non-threatening and feeling person. Don't pretend it doesn't exist, but get it out in front of you so you can deal with it in a constructive way.

THE PHYSICAL SITUATION, THE ON-SITE INSPECTION

If you have ever tried to speak in a room where there was a howling baby or a happy drunk, you know what I mean when I speak about distraction. You cannot build rapport with your audience without having their full attention, and whatever distracts them from you is a hindrance to your experiencing Charis-magic power.

Some of my most difficult speaking engagements were situations where I was at the mercy of the circumstances around me. The degree to which you can reduce outside disruptions will add to your getting through to your audience with power.

Here are some "nuts-and-bolts" suggestions to help you minimize the possibility of something going wrong with your speech:

Arrive at the meeting early enough to check out the situation for yourself. Let your guest know that you have arrived so he can set his mind at ease.

Ask to meet the person introducing you. You might be surprised to find out that for some reason he didn't get your prepared Introduction and was just planning to jot down a few notes.

Give him the extra Introduction you brought with you and go over it with him, adjusting it in any way appropriate for that particular meeting. Stress how important he is in helping you set the stage for your speech.

Ask to see where you'll be speaking. I'm not the shortest man in the world, but I've been put behind my share of lecterns that have hit me right under my nose. You really can't generate too much Charis-magic power with your audience if all they can see is a pair of eyes peering out from behind the mums.

Clear away as much as possible from in front of you. Anything that gets between you and your audience is a form of psychological barrier. The most ideal situation is to have nothing in front of you except a microphone so you can communicate with your entire body. This suggestion might seem a little far-fetched for you at this time, but work toward it as a Charis-magic ideal.

Check the sound system. Will you be wearing a lapel mike or using a stand-up mike? If you are going to be in motion, make certain the cord is sufficiently long enough to go with you. Nothing is quite as distracting as seeing a speaker trying to reach a blackboard that is just out of the reach of his microphone cord. Many smaller meeting rooms use small, self-contained battery powered systems. Check it. If the batteries are low, you are in for some problems.

Find out where the speakers are located and where your sound will be coming from. Most large rooms have a series of small overhead speakers scattered systematically in the ceiling. They can be very deceptive because you cannot tell from the podium how well you are amplifying. Get someone to stand out on the stage and speak, and you go into the auditorium or room and listen for yourself.

One of the worst situations for sound that I ever encountered was a meeting set in a gymnasium. They tried to use the bullhorns mounted in the center and they so distorted my voice, that I ended up trying to speak to a thousand people by shouting in their direction.

Sound is extremely critical and I would fight to get the best possible system working for you. What good is all your preparation if nobody's going to hear you?

Listen for distractions. Are the heating units noisy? Will there be another meeting going on in the room next to yours at the same time? If you are speaking at a banquet will the waiters be trying to clear the tables while you are speaking? Don't try it; there's no way you can win. If they insist on clearing, wait for the waiters to finish.

Check the seating arrangement. Remember the principle that heat generates heat. The closer people are together, the easier it is to build rapport with them as an audience. If the chairs are movable, have them arranged in such a way that you are as close to the people as physically possible. You might consider placing them in a semi-circle or filling in any empty space between you and the first row. Make sure that you will not have any major obstructions like support columns between you and the audience.

Try to limit the number of seats available to the number of people expected. Last year I was invited to conduct a half-day seminar for a Realtors' Board in Pennsylvania. The hotel had set up 275 seats and we had 110 registrations. We cleared out the extra seats. Consider the difference between 110 people drawn in tightly on top of one another and 110 people scattered loosely around an audience. The first situation generates rapport; the second, a feeling of "where is everybody?"

If you are speaking at a banquet, remember that most of the people are sitting at tables with their backs to you. Ask the chairman to have them turn their seats around and face the platform before you speak.

If you are planning to use props, be sure to check out the electrical sockets, lighting, equipment, etc. in advance. We all have had our share of someone stumbling around in the dark trying to get his slides turned right-side up. When it comes to audio-visual aids, the saying is true, "if anything can happen, it will!"

And last of all, here's a profound piece of advice I got from a man who has been a professional speaker for more years than I can count—always find out where the nearest rest room is located.

THE AUDIENCE EXPECTATION, FINDING THEIR PULSE

Every meeting is permeated by a prevailing mood of some kind. Even as individuals can experience all kinds of feelings, so an audience can reflect differing temperaments.

Two meetings at which I spoke back to back come to mind immediately. The first was the annual banquet of a large manufacturing firm. That week, the employees had learned that the company had gone into receivership and their mood that night was very evident. Their concern over their jobs and the future hung like a heavy cloud over the banquet. I knew that whatever my message that night, I had to include some words of encouragement.

The next night, I walked into a different world; the annual meeting of a national sports association meeting at Disney World. Sportsmen and sportswomen from all over the United States had gathered and the mood was festive and buoyant. I could have read recipes that night and they would have cheered me on!

Dr. Charles Jarvis, a dentist turned humorist, commented in a recent seminar on the subject of humor, that much of his success depends on getting the audience into a mood he calls "in fun." This is a warm state of mind where they are receptive to the flow of humor and get into the spirit of having a good time.

If you are going to communicate with persuasive power, you need to be alert to these moods and take them into consideration in your presentations. One of the ways you can "tune in" to your audience is to meet them before you speak.

Take advantage of any receptions or gatherings of the audience before your speaking engagement. Here you can begin to build the trust relationship that sets the foundation for a Charis-magic speech. In this informal setting, people can come to know you as a *friendly* and non-threatening person, and you can begin to set in motion the assurances of being a *caring* and *sincere* speaker.

Every person you can meet before the fact will be one less source of audience resistance when you get up to speak. Go after winning your audience one at a time and start your momentum going before you ever say a word from the podium. This technique has been one of the strictest practices of my own speaking approach. I always arrive early to get to know the people I am called on to serve, and, if possible, stay late to enjoy them as individuals.

Sometimes I run into some strange situations. I was called on to do a series of seminars for a highly technically-oriented industry. The employees were to leave their shifts to come to the auditorium for the session. I asked to be at the door to meet them, only to find that I had been escorted to a kitchen. My host pointed to a door; "The employees will be gathering in the room in there. After they get settled I'll take you out and introduce you."

". . . but I want to go out now and meet them," I insisted.

". . . but our speakers never meet the people before they speak."

"Well, this one does, You can stay here with the pots and pans if you want, but I've come to do business, and I won't sit here and lose the opportunity to get to know my audience. You want my best, and my best means "tuning in" to the people."

Meeting the members of your audience before you speak also gives you the opportunity to *look for the "trophy case,"* to find some example of group pride that you can work into your opening remarks to help build rapport. You will also get a chance to "test the water" to find out how good a job has been done in building your *audience expectation* for your coming.

If the people recognize your name immediately as one of the speakers and make some comment about your subject, "I have always been interested in motivation . . ." then you know some groundwork has been laid; on the other hand, if you keep having to explain who you are and what you are doing here, you know you have your work cut out for you.

Meeting your audience before you address them will also open up the possibility that you will be able to find a *power Closing,* some story, some incident that happened, some shared comments by one of the people. *Look for the power story!* Ask questions like "How long have you been with the company?" and "What do you feel about the people you work with?" Somewhere in that crowd is someone who has the story to enrich your Closing with Charis-magic power.

Some speakers disagree with me at this point about mixing with the audience. They feel that they should be inaccessible before they speak; and so they wait until the last minute to make their entrance. As far as I'm concerned, they might as well have sent their tape recorder for all the good they will do to meet the needs of their audience.

The name of this game is POWER!, and power comes from your ability as a speaker to build trust by feeling the pulse and needs of your audience and directing your message to zero in on "where the people live."

THE ACTUAL PRESENTATION, CHARIS-MAGIC POWER IN MOTION

We have spent much time together in this book preparing the bow, *the speaker,* and the arrow, *the speech;* and now comes the time for the bow to send the arrow winging toward the target, *the audience.*

The arrow is being placed in the bow . . . Your Introduction is being made. Listen to it carefully if it is not your own. See if it is establishing your right to speak and showing that you know what you are talking about, or if you're going to have to shore it up in your opening remarks.

You may feel a little nervous, but probably more excited than anything else. If you feel your heart pounding, pant like a little puppy in short, rapid-fire breaths that will force loads of oxygen into your system and quiet you down. This is much more effective than the classic advice, "take a deep breath."

Fill your mind with *high expectations* and sense that something good and unusual is going to happen. Feel the *self-confidence* that vibrates through your body as you think about your speech. You feel good about it! You know exactly how you are going to start, and you have a well-constructed Unit outline that leaves you *flexible* and open to change.

Your *support material* is relevant and personal and you have scattered *"bits and pieces"* of yourself as *knowledgeable, friendly, sincere* and *caring* throughout your content in order to build a *trust relationship* with your audience.

You think about your *Closing* and you feel good about it. Clearly it wraps up your *purpose,* and brings a *benefit* to your audience and sets out a course of *action* for them.

The Introduction is coming to a close now. Your first critical moments are now; *the arrow is being drawn back into the bow.* You are announced and you get up to move to the podium. Some rush at it like a bull after a waving cape and you can't help but feel there's something a little aggressive about someone who charges at you.

Move *naturally* and approach the podium with an easy smile and normal gestures. There's so much talk about gestures and how to do them; just move the way you would naturally in a non-speaking situation—just *be yourself!*

Look your audience in the eye; how critical this move is. People feel they can't trust someone who can't look them in the eye. They have been conditioned to believe that someone with shifty eyes can't be trusted. How many times have you heard, "I like a man who can look me in the eyes?"

Let the audience feel the power of your personal presence before you say a word. Look them in the eyes, stand tall but don't be arrogant. You are not some slave bent over with eyes cast to the ground because you are not allowed to look at your masters; you are a bearer of good news, a person who has come to share a benefit with another human being. Use strong eye contact! Let the audience feel the power of your presence through just a look!

You speak, *the arrow is in flight now, moving toward its target!* Your *opening remarks* are warm, friendly, related to the people and they sense immediately that you are *not a threat* to them. Your *content* begins to unfold; strong *Units* of power, well-constructed with relevant *support material*, enhancing, explaining and driving home the *points* you want to make. You share "*bits and pieces*" of yourself throughout your presentation and work through the *audience resistance* turning them into *trusting friends.*

You sense somewhere into your speech that suddenly they are yours, you "*own the crowd.*" They are open and receptive to the final impact of your message, and it comes swiftly, like the winging arrow, in the *Closing story*, a warm, personal and powerful instance of the kind of stuff that life is made of . . . *the arrow hits the bull's-eye!*

Your Charis-magic power as a speaker vibrates through the audience, through their bodies and feet and hands. They just can't sit there without expressing in some way their thanks to you for touching their lives, their appreciation that you have been more than another rubber-chicken, after-dinner speaker, their understanding of what it takes as a person to expose and share "bits and pieces" of yourself.

For what is a *standing ovation* but the most natural response of an audience to a speaker who has taken a chance to get his message through? By standing and applauding, the audience is revealing and returning to you an intimate insight into their own personal lives and the kind of people they are.

The audience is saying "amen and amen" to the values and feelings you have exposed and shared, and now they are trying to tell you, "you are our kind of person!"

Charis-magic—no power like it, no exhilaration to match it, no greater affirmation of what we are as flesh and blood human beings! *Charis-magic:* the power to move people!

Your Preparation, The Physical Situation, The Audience Expectation, The Actual Presentation, all are important to the final desired result, a Charis-magic presentation. Stay with this chapter. Read it over several times, and make a habit of reading it immediately before every one of your speaking engagements. Let the chapter serve as a check list to determine how well you have prepared yourself and your material, and to help you on the site to clear away possible distractions and "tune in" to the mood of your audience.

We have come close to the end of this book, but there is one final question to be answered; "Where is the source of energy, vitality, enthusiasm, that seems to mark the Charis-magic speaker?" What is his "secret" of inner power flow that seems to energize his speeches beyond some simple explanation of "think positive." In the chapter to follow I will be sharing some personal thoughts on that intriguing question.

 Twelve

Unleashing
Charis-Magic Energy

The great chefs of the past would protect their culinary creations by one of two methods; either by refusing to give the recipe to the person requesting it, or by freely sharing the recipe with anyone who asked for it but always leaving out the one ingredient that would turn the collection of hodge-podge foods and spices into a rare eating delicacy.

Without the "secret" ingredient, the promising dish would turn out to be just another meal, but when it was added—synergism! The meal became greater than all its ingredients.

Sometimes when a person comes to the close of a book such as this one with so many "bits and pieces," suggestions, steps to take, helps to follow, he might have an uneasy feeling that somewhere, somehow, something has been left out, some ingredient that brings it all together in a cohesive and powerful conclusion.

This chapter is dedicated to uncovering that "secret" ingredient! At this point, more than ever before in this book, you will be entering the arena of my own personal opinions and reflections. Take them, filter them through the screens of your own reasoning and experiences, and accept them for what they might be worth to you. Thank you for considering them.

PERSONAL REFLECTIONS ON CHARIS-MAGIC POWER

In the Introduction to this book I defined *charisma* as "that rare quality that is attributed to people who have a dynamic leadership ability and who inspire great loyalty and devotion in others," and *magic* as "the power to produce effects that seem more than human." The Charis-magic speaker, then, is a person who possesses certain qualities that draw people to him like magic in a trusting relationship.

During the course of this book we have diagnosed some of these qualities in terms of certain assurances, but now we reach for an almost indefinable quality, the quality of magnetism, or enthusiasm, or vitality, or, what I have come to call, ENERGY! It is this non-verbal communication of restless energy that lies at the core of the Charis-magic speaker.

Slowly, through the years, I have come to the conclusion that the source of this tremendous energy found in certain people comes from their deep sense of purpose in life; purpose that is larger than the moment, greater than any one part of the universe, towering over man's lumbering mentality; purpose that so permeates their very fiber as a human being, that you cannot separate them or their words from their sense of mission.

A Sense Of Purpose: People are drawn to those who move with a sense of certainty. They are always looking for stability in a shaky world and assurances amid so many question marks. The Charis-magic personality is marked by strong "vibes" of purpose and direction. The Charis-magic speaker points people unashamedly and boldly to certainties about himself and his message. Where there is no sense of purpose, a speaker falters and a life drowns in shallow water.

Right after I finished speaking at an industrial meeting in Boston, a man approached me and asked if I'd meet him in the Coffee Shop a little later. During that meeting, he gave me a rare insight into a person's life.

"Do you remember how you were talking about finding purpose in your work and about how it would make a difference in your life and feelings of usefulness?"

I told him I recalled that part of my speech and elaborated on some additional feelings of mine. He listened intently and then said, "I want to share something that happened to me with you.

"About seven years ago I started to take a hard look at my life. I had taken a little company and worked my gut out to make it the success it is today, but one morning I got up and wondered what I was knocking myself out for.

"I was fed up with the business, fed up with the grind; all I wanted to do was just throw it all over and give up. Now, I don't mean just give up my business, I felt like giving up on life. I thought about it a long time and finally decided my life didn't have any purpose or direction anymore, and I decided to kill myself.

"I was sitting in my office brooding about it when a salesman came by to show me some products. I had known him a few years and for some reason I started to tell him about how I felt and what I was thinking, and he stopped me right in the middle and said, 'I don't care about you and your problems. I'm too busy!' and he turned around and walked out.

"I figured I had just gotten a good taste of what life was really like, just plain dog-eat-dog, so I took my gun out of my desk and drove down to the shore to end it. I stood there and finally put the gun to my head and just before I pulled the trigger I thought to myself, 'You know, you do have one other option. You can go back to your job and just go through the motions every day and just pretend that your life has purpose and some meaning."

He looked at me with a mixture of sadness and melancholy longing as though he were trying to find something to anchor himself to. "You know something? For seven years now, I've been getting up every day and pretending that life has meaning for me."

Enthusiasm is a powerful word, coming from the ancient Green en-theos, and literally meaning "in-god" or "to be possessed by a god." The word was used in this ancient past to describe those persons who were so filled with the excitement of life and the possession of energy that they were considered to be possessed.

They saw purpose and meaning in everything around them. Their lives had purpose, their jobs had purpose, the universe itself was permeated with purpose. They lived *enthusiastically*. When life is filled with that sense of purpose, when you are able to shout into the vastness of the universe and it answers that there is meaning in everything you do, then your life is energized; and that energy permeates every fiber of your body, mind and spirit.

The Charis-magic speaker is marked by his own conviction that his message is a good and worthwhile one and his life is filled with purpose in sharing it.

Sincerity Has No Substitute: If a good speech is marked by a man having a message, then a Charis-magic speech is marked by the *message having the man!* His speech is wrapped in his own personal convictions. He believes what he is saying and backs up those beliefs with all the qualities of what he is as a person. His message cannot be held in. Like some "fire in his bones" he feels almost compelled to share it, and the audience cannot help but sense it in the air and see it in his eyes.

In an earlier chapter, we discussed the assurance of *sincerity* as a necessary condition for building trust with the audience. Now, I am pressing the case even further by insisting that a speaker should not only *appear* to be sincere, he should in truth be a person who *is* sincere, a person who appears "without wax."

His message should be an extension of himself, an eruption out of the very core of his personal convictions. A case might be made that this is not necessarily so, that many speakers "get away with murder" by *pretending* to be sincere and caring. I can see the logic in that argument because I meet professional speakers who do their same bit time and time again with no personal regard for the people or any personal commitment to the content of their speeches.

On the surface then, it might appear that being sincere

has no edge in the power arena of speaking; but that's on the surface. If you remember the story I shared on the background of the word "sincere", you will recall that it referred to those craftsmen who created their sculptures sin-cere, without wax; that is, they refused to cover up a mistake in their work by filling the flaw in with wax and selling it to the public as a perfect piece of sculpture.

Now, let me tell you the rest of that story. The people of the day were becoming suspicious of the works of the artists, so they devised a test that would show them if the work was genuine and was what it appeared to be, or if it was filled with flaws covered over by wax.

The questionable piece of art would be placed in the sun and the heat of the burning rays would be allowed to bake it. Under that unrelenting pressure, the piece would soon be exposed for what it was—either genuine or with melting wax showing all the flaws.

A speaker may be appearing to "pretend his way through" but when the time of heat and pressure comes, when he is tested to see what he really is, then the flaws will be exposed. There's an old saying that's also a powerful reminder, something about, "You can fool all the people some of the time and . . ."

Powerful and persuasive speaking comes from a blend of the message and the messenger. In the terms of an analogy I heard some years ago, Charis-magic power can be experienced by a speaker who has knowledge and skills on the one hand and personal integrity and sincerity on the other. When you know something, it's just like having a glove on one of your hands, and when you are something, it's like having a glove on the other hand. Being a public speaker is a two-fisted adventure; if you're going to score a knockout, you had better go into the ring with both gloves on!

A Service To Others: Among my many memories related to my experiences in direct sales is a lingering moment at a sales meeting. On that particular day the boss had brought in a guest speaker who came to give us a "pep talk," and what a talk it was. I can vividly see him jumping up and down on the chairs, throwing his jacket in the air and bellowing, "Ya got to go if you're gonna grow!"

He talked about enthusiasm, getting excited, and never taking "no" for an answer. He cajoled, pleaded, promised, and worked us over until, when he finally finished, I felt as if I had been strained through a sieve. Our boss got up immediately and said, "If you jokers could get as excited about your job as he is about his, you wouldn't be able to bank the money fast enough!"

Over the years I've thought about that incident and what it means to get excited about something. What I have concluded is that excitement in the area of selling something, whether it is a camera or an idea in a speech, comes from a burning belief that you have something that will be so good for someone, that you can hardly wait to tell them about it.

Excitement and energy in public speaking do not necessarily show themselves by arm waving, or jumping up and down or shouting at the top of the voice. Genuine power and Charis-magic energy manifest themselves in a dedicated belief in your message, and a burning desire to get it to others so they can enjoy the *benefits* you have to offer.

The Charis-magic speaker is marked by his conviction that what he has to say is so filled with the potential of touching lives and helping others, he can't wait to share it. Speaking, for him, becomes a *service to others*, an opportunity to enrich their lives, lift their spirits, give them a better standard of living, help educate their children, protect their future, improve their health, increase their income; any of one and a hundred possible ways to touch them on the level of their *human needs*.

I remember an architect friend who had become bored with his work and his many achievements. His days became filled with drudgery and his work had lost its vitality and creativity. I lost touch with him for a few years and the next time I saw him he was a changed man. His life pulsated with energy and vitality and he fairly burst with excitement in his work.

What made the difference? He had given up his designing of massive shopping centers and office buildings and had started to specialize in designing children's wards in hospitals. For the first time in his professional career he felt in touch with human life and saw his talents as helping and caring.

The speaker who moves from simply putting together a well-designed and structured presentation to feeling that he is involved in the adventure of touching human lives will discover reserves of power and energy.

Seeing your speaking as a service to others, an opportunity to be involved in "the kinds of things that life is made of" will return some unanticipated rewards. Take the example of a very special man:

Gathering Living Trophies: I was invited to be a guest for the weekend at Joe's home in North Carolina; a beautiful setting, near the coast, in a small rural town of very gracious people. Joe told me that years before when he was working out of New Jersey covering his insurance territory as a manager, he had driven through the town with his wife and had turned to her and said,

"When we retire, I'm going to build a home right here. I just want to get away from the rat race and this seems like a little bit of heaven to me."

. . . and he did! In the midst of towering pines, dogwoods and azaleas, he built a lovely two-story home.

Early, my first morning, I got up and slipped quietly downstairs to the kitchen to get a cup of coffee. I thought I was the first one up, but, to my surprise, Joe was sitting at the kitchen table, reading the morning newspaper and enjoying a cup of hot brew.

I slipped into a chair and poured myself a cup and for a few moments we just sat in silence enjoying the beauty of that Carolina morning. The sliding doors of the kitchen were open and the fragrance of the dogwoods just seemed to fill the room.

I finally broke the silence. "Joe, tell me, how do you summarize your life? How do you evaluate all the work you have done and what filters down to you now as really being important as you look back over all the years?"

He thought for a long moment and then commented, "You know, Dick, when I was a young man just starting out in the insurance business, I attended a convention in Atlantic City. I still remember it as though it were yesterday. I was walking down a hall and I heard two men talking about their manager who had suffered a heart attack and died the day before, and one of the men said,

'The s.o.b. should have died twenty years ago!'

"I couldn't believe it. How could they talk about a human life that way? And then I wondered what would be said in summary of my life by those I would have worked with. That's stayed on my mind a lot of years now."

He seemed to fade away from me, his mind reliving the events of the past. I sat quietly and before long he returned and continued expressing his feelings.

"You know something, Dick, I'm so glad I've got some living trophies."

"That's a new concept to me, Joe, I'm afraid I don't know what you mean by living trophies." Again he seemed to drift away in his thoughts, and then he said,

"Dick, all the trophies I received during all those 37 years with the company are rusting in the attic, and all the certificates and commendations I got are yellowing with age, but I've got living trophies, people that I've helped along the way, people that I've serviced, and young men that I helped in the company to become more than I ever became . . . LIVING TROPHIES!

"You know, I've got more money than I need and more house than I can use. I could wish my wife's health was a little better; she won't even be able to come down this morning, she's feeling so badly. But do you want to know what makes it all worth the living in these last days of my life?

"Hearing from one of my trophies, having him call me on the phone and ask, 'How are you doing Joe?' or getting a Christmas card from one of them, or having one of them come through town and stop by and introduce me to his wife and kids.

"You know, it would be a sad and lonely life for me if I hadn't spent a little time along the way to gather up a few living trophies."

Being a public speaker offers some rewarding experiences—the applause, the ovations, the adulation, the admiration; but nothing surpasses the greatest moment of all, to touch a life and find a living trophy!

ENERGY, the ingredient that energizes the Charis-magic speaker, is rooted in his sense of purpose, his sincerity, and his service to others through his presentations. When these factors are alive in him and he adds growing knowledge and developing skills, he can move people with Charis-magic power!

CHARIS-MAGIC IN PUBLIC SPEAKING: AN OVERVIEW AND SUMMARY

My search for the secret of persuasive power led me to conclude that persuasive power depends on the speaker's expectation of power (Chapter One) and his ability to build a trust relationship between himself and his audience (Chapter Two).

Studies show that this trust relationship depends on the audience's receiving certain "vibes" or assurances that convince them that the speaker is: (Chapter Three)

- a warm and open person who poses no threat (Chapter Four)
- an expert in his field who knows what he is talking about (Chapter Five)
- sincere and can be believed (Chapter Six)
- concerned about each person (Chapter Seven)
- bringing a message that has a benefit (Chapter Eight)

The impressions or assurances lead to persuasive power; the stronger the impressions, the greater the trust.

A persuasive speaker, therefore, must build into his speech those elements that will produce these "vibes" or assurances. He will use those techniques, methods, and materials that will generate the impression that he is friendly, knowledgeable, sincere, caring, and brings a benefit.

This is done in the speech preparation stage by the structuring of the speech (Chapter Nine) and the selection of the support material (Chapter Ten), and in the delivery stage by the actual presentation (Chapter Eleven).

All of this is energized into actuality by a speaker who is marked by purpose, sincerity and service to others (Chapter Twelve).

The End Result: a speaker mentally prepared to expect power, a speech prepared to persuade in a particular direction, an audience prepared to receive persuasion, and the generating of a *relationship of trust* between the speaker and the audience that makes it possible to persuade; the end result, Charis-magic power.

 Thirteen

A
Charis-Magic
Treasure Chest

This collection of anecdotes and motivational and humorous stories are intended to be samples of the kinds of materials that can spice up and drive home important points in your presentation. The majority of them are humorous in nature. The intent is to show that useful illustrations are always available if you develop the eyes to see them.

The headings are intended to show you a situation or application that can be made of the illustration. This is only a single suggestion. Other uses can readily be discovered as you ponder the point of the story.

A Personal Note: These stories have not been plucked out of the air to fill the pages, but have been carefully distilled out of a lifetime of exposure to thousands of bits of material. For every one that I have included, there are twenty others that were discarded. Enjoy them, use them, and let them energize your presentations with vitality and Charis-magic power:

APPLYING ADVICE

Late one afternoon, a man went out walking along a mountain path that was new to him. Without a warning, he stepped too close to the edge of a sharp precipice and slipped off. As he was tumbling down to certain doom he somehow managed to grab hold of a branch and he held on for dear life. He dangled there in space for what seemed an eternity and then looked up to the heavens and prayed, "Oh, Lord, can anyone up there help me?"

To his amazement a voice came back, "Yes, I am up here and I can help you. Do you have faith in me?"

The man yelled back, "Oh, yes, Lord, I do, You know I do!"

The voice then commanded, "Okay, then let go of the branch and I will save you."

There was a long pause and then the man yelled back, "Is there anyone else up there who can help me?"

ATTENTION TO DETAIL

Some years ago we lost a rocket that was headed for a probe of the planet Venus. The cost of the project was $18,500,000 and we lost every penny because someone forgot a hyphen.

During the launch, the rocket went slightly off course which was predicted and expected, and the programmer was suppose to feed the computer a hyphen or bar in the instructions to tell the computer not to worry, that everything was normal.

But the hyphen was missing and the computer started making all kinds of adjustments that it shouldn't have, thinking the rocket was off course. The end result—the rocket had to be destroyed.

An ironic story—that a rocket primed for a trip of 180-million miles stumbled over something the size of a pin head.

BUSINESS ETHICS

A very hard-nosed businessman was involved in a heated discussion with one of his competitors whom he disliked over how to carry out their business. The words were flying between them at a fevered pitch until the businessman finally exploded,

"I'll tell you something for sure—there are lots of ways to make a pile of money in our work, but there is only one honest way!"

"Only one honest way," repeated the puzzled competitor, "and what is it?"

"Aha, just as I suspected all along," sneered the first man, "You don't know!"

COMMUNICATION: CREATIVE, CONFUSED AND TACTFUL

Creative Communication: American companies that are required to make transatlantic telephone calls have come up with an idea that has cut the cost of their calls to a minimum. They record their messages on a tape recorder, accelerate the speed and play it over the phone to another recorder on the other end. Then that recorder is played at the reduced speed and the messages are delivered intact. How about that for American ingenuity?

Confused Communication: The church governing board was in a heated discussion. A member of the congregation had recommended that a chandelier be placed in the foyer of the new sanctuary being planned. The debate raged hot and furious for over an hour until one old-timer rose to his feet and asked to be heard.

"I'm opposed to this motion for two reasons," he began. "In the first place, we've done pretty well in this church for over fifty years without a chandelier, and in the second place, if we buy it, we don't have a person in this congregation who can play it."

Tactful Communication: Harry Truman liked to tell a story about one of his speeches that he had delivered at a Grange Convention in Kansas City. In the audience that particular day was Mrs. Bess Truman and a friend of hers. In his speech, Truman told the delegates, "I grew up on a farm and one thing I'm sure about—farming means manure, manure, and more manure."

Down in the audience, Mrs. Truman's friend leaned over to her and said, "Bess why on earth can't you get Harry to say 'fertilizer'?"

To which Mrs. Truman replied. "Good Lord, Helen, it's taken me thirty years to get him to say 'manure'!"

Tactful Communication: After one of his speeches, a well-known speaker was approached by a little, silver-haired lady who expressed how much pleasure she had gotten from his remarks.

"I took the opportunity to speak to you," she said quietly, "because you said in your speech that you loved old ladies."

"I do," he said smiling at her, "and I also like them your age."

CLOSING A SALE

An enterprising insurance agent told his new prospect, "I'm not like some other insurance agents you might have dealt with. I want to sell you this policy, but I'm not going to try and scare you into buying it. Why don't you just sleep on it and if you wake up in the morning give me a call."

CREATIVE MARKETING: GIVING ADDED VALUE

A particular young salesgirl in a candy store always had a line of customers waiting for her to wait on them while other girls just stood around doing nothing.

The owner of the store was puzzled by the situation and finally took the girl aside to ask her the reason for her popularity.

"It's really very simple," she replied, "All the other girls scoop up more than a pound of candy and then have to take some off the scales, but I always scoop up less than a pound and end up having to add to it."

CRITICISM: LISTENING TO

A farmer came to town and asked the owner of a large seafood restaurant if he could use a thousand frog's legs. The owner was surprised and asked the farmer where he could get so big a haul.

"I've got a pond back home that's just packed with them," he replied. "They drive me crazy all night with their loud croaking."

They agreed on a price and the owner ordered two hundred legs. A week later the farmer returned with two scrawny frogs and a foolish grin on his face.

"I guess I was wrong," the farmer said sheepishly. "There were only two of them in the pond, but boy could they make a lot of noise!"

A father and his son decided to take one of their donkeys to the market place to sell. As they set out on their trip the father got on the donkey and the son walked beside him. Soon they met several people coming from the other direction and heard one say, "He should be ashamed of himself—a strong man like him riding on the donkey while his poor little boy walks." So the father got off and the son got on the donkey.

It wasn't long until they met some other people and heard them say, "How can this be? Look at that young boy sitting on the donkey while his old father is forced to walk." So they both got on the donkey only to hear some other strangers say, "Shame on those two, sitting on the back of one little donkey, Don't they have any heart?"

So they both got off and walked only to hear, "How stupid. The donkey has nothing on his back and they are both walking." Do you know how they finally arrived at the market?

They were both carrying the donkey!

DISAGREEMENTS

You should be tolerant of another person's right to disagree with you. After all, he certainly has a right to his ridiculous opinion.

ECONOMY: HARD TIMES

A man was awakened from his sleep in the middle of the night by the sounds of a prowler in his room.

"What are you looking for?" he whispered cautiously.

"Money!" the burglar growled.

"Wait a minute," the man shot back, "I'll get my pants on and help you look!"

"How's business these days?" asked Joe.

"It's terrible! Couldn't be worse. Even my customers who never pay their bills have stopped buying."

In Tokyo, a used-car salesman put a sign out in front of his business; "We pay highest prices for cars we buy. We get lowest prices for cars we sell. How we stay in business? We lucky!"

A man wrote the loan company he was doing business with, "Thank you for the money. I will be eternally in your debt."

EXCUSE MAKING

The billing department of a Florida Utility Company recently reported some of the excuses they had received from their customers for not paying their water bills:

"Somebody stole my mailbox . . ."

"How could we possibly use that much water? My husband and I shower together . . ."

"The skating rink next door is using my water. I made a deal with them. Haven't they paid you yet?"

"My son ate the bill."

A man stopped at a farmer's house and asked to borrow his axe.

"I'm sorry," the farmer said, "I'm going to town this afternoon and I can't lend you my axe."

"But what has that got to do with lending me your axe?" the puzzled borrower asked.

"Well, sir," the farmer replied, "when you don't want to do something, one excuse is as good as another."

EXPERT

The young pilot of a riverboat on the mighty Mississippi was bragging about his skill to a nervous passenger. "Don't worry," he assured him, "I've been piloting boats on this river so long that I know every snag, every log and every sandbar there is."

Just then the boat struck a submerged obstacle with such force that the boat shivered from stem to stern and felt as if it was going to fall apart.

"There," said the pilot matter-of-factly, "that's one of them now."

FIRST IMPRESSIONS

You never get a second chance to make a first impression.

FOLLOWING INSTRUCTIONS

The sergeant of the guard put a raw recruit on duty for the first time at the gate to the post with the instructions not to let any car through that didn't have a window sticker.

The first automobile to drive up contained a high-ranking

officer and his private chauffeur, but there wasn't a sticker on the window.

"Halt!" the recruit shouted.

The officer instructed his chauffeur to keep on going and to ignore the command.

"Begging your pardon, sir," the recruit said, "I'm kind of new at this. Whom do I shoot first, you or the driver?"

GET IT IN WRITING

The young man had gotten himself into a financial mess. He had lent a friend $250 but he didn't get a note, a receipt or an IOU of any kind to prove it. He needed his money back but now faced the fact he had nothing to show for his loan. He finally went to his father for help.

After hearing the story his father told him, "Write your friend a letter and ask for the $500 you lent him. Tell him you need it right now."

"But I only loaned him $250," the puzzled son replied.

"I know that, but you say $500 and he'll write you back that he only owes you $250 and then you'll have it in writing."

GETTING THE ORDER: AN ANCIENT PARABLE

Now it came to pass that a great traveler approached a herd of donkeys and asked, "What would a donkey need for a three-day journey into the wilderness?"

And they answered him, "Six bundles of hay and three bags of dates." And he replied, "That sounds fair enough, but I only need one of you. Who will go for less?"

So behold, one donkey said he would go for six bundles of hay and two bags of dates. Another said five bundles of hay and one bag of dates; but one donkey brayed, "I'll go for just one bundle of hay."

The other donkeys exclaimed, "You are a disgrace to the donkey business and stupid at that. Thou knowest no donkey can survive for three days on a bundle of hay much less clear any kind of profit."

"I know," whined the donkey, hanging his long ears in shame, "but I wanted the order!"

GOVERNMENT ASSISTANCE

The chicken farmer was losing a lot of his flock, and, hoping to solve his problem, he wrote the Department of Agriculture:

"Gentlemen, something is seriously wrong with my chickens. Every morning when I get up I find three or four of them lying on their backs. Their bodies are cold and stiff and their legs are straight up in the air. What's wrong with them?"

Three months later he got his reply from Washington, "Dear sir," it read, "after due deliberation and consultation with our experts we have come to the conclusion that your chickens are dead."

HANDLING ROUTINE WORK ON THE JOB

A man was driving down a country road and was surprised to see a farmer plowing his field with a bull dragging the plow. He stopped his car and walked over to the fence where the farmer had paused to rest for a spell.

"You know," the stranger said, "I'm not trying to tell you how to run your farm, but you sure could get a lot more done in a lot shorter time if you had a tractor."

The farmer chewed on a straw for a long moment and then said, "I got a tractor. Just don't want to use it."

"Why not?" the stranger asked.

"Well mister," the farmer drawled," I just wanted this bull to find out that life ain't all romance."

HARD EMPLOYER

The old-time plumber was worried about all the time that was lost on the job with coffee breaks, featherbedding, gabbing and other interruptions.

"When I was an apprentice," he said, "we used to lay down the first two lengths of pipe. Then the boss would turn on the water and we would have to stay ahead of it."

And then there was the boss who was so mean he gave his employee a raise before he fired him so he would be losing a better job.

HEALTH

A speaker at the National Congress of Mental Health gave this description of the modern executive:

"There are four types of executives: First of all, there is the Ulceroidal type, who is always worrying about the problem. Second, there is the Thyroidal type who tries to run around the problem. Third, there is the Adenoidal type who yells and screams about the problem; and Fourth, there is the Hemorrhoidal type, who sits on it and waits for it to clear up."

A political prisoner in South America was about to be executed by a firing squad. He was led outside the prison to a wall and blindfolded. The Captain of the execution detail asked him if he wanted a last cigarette.

"No thank you," said the doomed prisoner, "I'm trying to quit."

A concerned Doctor told his carousing, young patient, "The best thing for you to do is give up smoking, drinking, and women."

To which his patient replied, "I really don't deserve the best, Doc, What's second best?"

INEFFECTIVE METHODS

Two Indians sat by the ocean for weeks watching the construction of a giant lighthouse. When it was finally finished, they anxiously waited to see it in operation. That first night they were standing there staring at it when a thick fog rolled in. They watched and listened for a while and finally one of them spoke:

"Ugh, light shine, bell ring, horn blow, but fog come in just the same."

INFLATION: RUNAWAY

The outrageous prices of today will probably be the dirt cheap bargains of tomorrow.

A man was in an automobile accident and went into a coma for twenty years. He finally awakened in 2010. After getting his bearings and being informed of his condition he excitedly called his stockbroker to see how his investments had done during his long absence. It took only a few minutes to discover that to his astonishment his 100 shares of A.T.&T were now worth 9-million dollars, his 200 shares of General Motors were worth 12-million dollars and his I.B.M. had soared to 20-million dollars.

"Good Lord," he cried out ecstatically, "I'm rich! I'm rich!"

At that moment, the telephone operator cut in and said, "Your three minutes are up, sir, Would you please deposit another million dollars?"

LOSING PERSONAL INDEPENDENCE

Several years ago, the shrimp boats that were fishing off the coast of St. Augustine, Florida moved to another location. Suddenly, the beaches were covered with the bodies of hundreds of dead seagulls. The residents were puzzled and set out to solve the mystery. The solution came as a subtle warning to all who give up their independence.

For years the gulls had been feeding on the unwanted shrimp that was thrown overboard by the fishing vessels each evening. In fact, they had become so dependent on this source of food that they had forgotten how to fish for themselves. They had traded in their self-sufficiency for the promise of someone else's carrying them through life. The end result was disaster.

LIE DETECTOR

Four boys decided to skip their early morning classes. They finally arrived at school after lunch and told the teacher they had a flat tire on the way and had trouble getting it repaired.

To their relief the teacher smiled pleasantly and said, "I'm sorry you had all that trouble, but I'm glad you finally got here. By the way, you missed a little quiz, so if you'll take some seats apart and get out some paper, I'll give it to you."

The boys quickly got into their places and readied themselves for the opening question. "That's fine," the teacher said, "Now answer this question: 'Which tire was flat?'"

LIMITATIONS

Somebody said it couldn't be done,
  but he with a grin replied,
"He'd never be one to say it couldn't be done,
  leastway, not 'til he tried."
So he buckled right in with a trace of a grin,
By golly, he went right to it.
He tackled the thing that couldn't be done,
  and he couldn't do it.

MAKING THE BEST OF A BAD SITUATION

A man had been bitten by a rabid dog and although the doctors had started treatment they weren't sure they had gotten to him in time. They decided to tell him that there was a chance he might develop hydrophobia and go out of his mind and die. One of the doctors gave him the bad news and was surprised to see the man start to write at great length.

After about an hour of this one of the nurses just had to ask him, "Are you writing your will, or maybe a letter to your family?"

"Nah, none of that," was his terse reply. "This is a list of the people I'm going to bite when I go mad."

MOTIVATING OTHERS

During World War I, the service was having trouble signing up men to take out the life insurance policy the government was writing on them. One Colonel was especially concerned that every man in his regiment be enrolled. He called in his top Sergeant and told him to talk to the men but not to put any undue pressure on them to sign up.

The Sergeant called the regiment together and explained, "Now men, most of you know me pretty well. We've worked together, eaten together, had some good times together. Now I want to give you a little advice.

Our government is going to have to pay out $10,000 every time an insured soldier is killed in battle, but they don't have to pay out a red cent if an uninsured man is killed.

Now think with me for a minute. Which of you soldiers do you think Uncle Sam is going to send to the front lines— those who are insured or those who are uninsured?"

OVERCOMING OBSTACLES

Carved into one of the buildings on the campus of the Massachusettes School for the Blind is this motto, "Obstacles are things to be overcome."

She was a frail little old lady who lived all by herself on the second floor of a boarding house. One fateful day she slipped on the stairs coming out of the house and ended up with a broken leg. She was rushed to the hospital where the Doctor put her leg into a cast and advised her, "Now don't go walking up and down those stairs until this leg of yours heals."

After several months, the Doctor finally removed the cast and the little old lady asked, "Doctor, is it all right to use the stairs now?"

"It certainly is" he replied.

"Thank the Lord," she sighed, "I'm plumb sick and tired of climbing up and down that danged drain pipe."

PLANNING

It takes just as much energy to plan as it does to hope.

Abraham Lincoln loved to tell the story about a young blacksmith who heated a piece of iron in his forge not knowing what he was going to do with it. First he thought he'd make a horseshoe, but in the middle of his hammering he changed his mind and started something else, only to change his mind again.

Before long, the iron was hammered in so many directions that it became useless. Holding it with his tongs the blacksmith looked at it with disgust and suddenly thrust it hissing into a tub of water.

"Well, he exclaimed, "at least I can make a big fizzle out of it."

POLLUTION

An Indian inhabitant of what is now called Mexico City was ordered hanged for the offense of burning charcoal in the city and polluting the air. The year was 1309 A.D.

PROCRASTINATION

The bartender had to come over to the customer who was getting noisy and out-of-hand and ask him to quiet down or get out. The man said, "Come on, have a little understanding. This is my 30th wedding anniversary."

"Oh, well," answered the bartender, "I guess you should enjoy yourself. Go ahead with your celebration."

"No you don't understand," the customer replied, "I'm drowning my sorrows."

"How come?" the puzzled bartender asked.

"Well you see, five years after I got married I was ready to murder my wife, but a lawyer friend persuaded me not to. He said I'd get 25 years in jail for it, and I was stupid enough to listen to him.

"What do you mean stupid," the bartender asked.

"Well, if I'd gone ahead with it, I'd be a free man today."

QUALITY OF WORK

"You talk about miserable work" the man complained to a friend, "They talked me into taking out stock in this company I work for and now I'm worried sick about the lousy work I'm turning out."

SALESMANSHIP

"Madam," said the door-to-door salesman to the lady of the house, "Do you mind if I show you a little item that your neighbor said you couldn't afford?"

SALARY

The job applicant was told by the executive, "We are looking for a good worrier; a person who can come in here every day and worry constructively. The job pays $500 a week. Do you want it?"

"You know I do," exclaimed the applicant, "but who will be paying me the $500?"

"Aha," said the executive, "that's your first worry."

SEEING OPPORTUNITY

Two shoe salesmen were sent to a remote part of the world to open a new market. A week after his arrival, the first salesman called his home office and told his boss with exasperation, "I'm coming home on the next plane. I can't sell any shoes here. Everyone is barefooted."

Nothing was heard from the second man until the home office received a wire with the message, "Fifty orders are on the way. More to follow. What a gold mine. Prospects are everywhere. No one has any shoes."

SELF-SUPPORT

Mildred Dilling relates an incident about Harpo Marx while he was one of her harp students. "Harpo was playing in a recital in my studio. When he finished and left the stage there was a long applause, but he didn't come back for an encore. Later I asked him why he had not responded to the tremendous applause of the audience."

"I couldn't," he told me, "I was out front helping to keep it going."

TAKING A CHALLENGE

Two old loggers in the Canadian wilds were comparing their strength and size. The little man was giving his big friend a hard time about his brawn. "Pierre, if I were as strong as you I'd go out in the woods and find me the biggest and most powerful bear out there and crush him with my bare hands."

Pierre smiled at his good friend and answered, "Jacque, there are a lot of small bears out there too."

TEAM EFFORT

Some years ago, two maritime officers, the captain and the chief engineer of the ship, were engrossed in a running argument as to which one of them was the most important to the running of the ship—the man who steered or the one who kept the boilers stoked.

After the argument had raged for several months, they decided to settle it by switching jobs for a day. The chief engineer went to the bridge and took over the wheel of the ship and the captain descended below to the boiler room to run the engines.

After a couple of hours, the captain climbed wearily up from the engine room. He was exhausted and covered in sweat and grease.

"Chief," he yelled, waving a monkey wrench, "you'll have to come down here and give me some help. I can't make this thing go."

"Of course you can't, you fool," bellowed the engineer, "she's aground!"

STICKING WITH THE JOB

The foreman of a crew loading cargo on a merchant ship was approached by a little man looking for work. He seemed desperate and pleaded, "I'll be glad to do anything. Just name it and I can do it."

The foreman was impressed with how earnest he was but

told him he wasn't big enough for the job, "We're loading anvils on this ship," he said. The little man insisted he could handle it and finally the foreman relented and put him on the crew. For the next few hours he watched in amazement as the little man carried anvil after anvil across the wooden plank into the hold of the ship.

Everything seemed to be progressing well until the inexperienced man slipped and fell overboard into the ocean. The workers rushed to the side of the ship and heard him yell, "Help, help, I can't swim!" and bobbed under. One of the men ran for a rope as he came to the surface again and yelled a second time, "Help, Help me. I'm drowning!" and then disappeared again. Just as they got ready to rescue him, he appeared for the third time and in a tone of exasperation and desperation yelled out, "So help me. If someone up there doesn't help me soon, I'm going to drop this anvil!"

TELLING IT LIKE IT IS: BUILDING CREDIBILITY

There is nothing like a good country-western song to tell it like it is. No problem of communication here. The words are clear and the message sings its way to the listener's ear: A few classic lines:

"She left me at Walgreens and I cried all the way to Sears . . ."
"Our marriage was a failure but our divorce ain't working out either . . ."
"I wouldn't take you to a dog fight, even if I thought you'd win . . ."
"When the phone don't ring, you'll know it's me . . ."
"If you want to keep the beer real cold, put it next to my ex-wife's heart . . ."
"I've got the hungries for your love and I'm waiting in the welfare line . . ."

TIME MANAGEMENT: DO IT NOW!

Suppose you had a bank that deposited 86,400 dollars to your account every morning on the condition that you could not carry over any of it to the next day; that any amount you failed to use would be cancelled out every evening. What would you do? Obviously, use every bit of it every day.

Every day you are credited with 86,400 seconds. None of it can be carried over. What you fail to invest and use you lose. Each day a new account is opened and each evening the records of the day are burned. Yesterday is the tomb of time, tomorrow in the womb. All you have is the present "now" to invest wisely.

The time has come for me to close. In the course of these pages I have given you my best and shared my personal convictions. I have purposely avoided gathering the "wisdom of the ages," but have gambled on my own experience and knowledge. Whatever else is to be said, at least let it be known that I "took a chance" and left "bits and pieces" of myself scattered throughout these pages.

Index